36480000007783

Women in Industry

Women in Industry

Employment Patterns of Women in Corporate America

Jerolyn R. Lyle
The American University

Jane L. Ross
U.S. Department of Health,
Education and Welfare

Lexington Books
D.C. Heath and Company
Lexington, Massachusetts
Toronto   London

Library of Congress Cataloging in Publication Data

Lyle, Jerolyn R.
  Women in industry.

  Bibliography: p.
  1. Woman—Employment—United States. 2. Discrimination in employment—United States. I. Ross, Jane L., joint author. II. Title.
HD6095.L94   331.4'0973   73-1012
ISBN 0-669-86124-3

Second printing, November 1974.

Published simultaneously in Canada.

Printed in the United States of America.

International Standard Book Number: 0-669-86124-3

Library of Congress Catalog Card Number: 73-1012

"The basis for self-esteem in a just society is not then one's income share but the publicly affirmed distribution of fundamental rights and liberties. And this distribution being equal, everyone has a similar and secure status when they meet to conduct the common affairs of the wider society."

John Rawls. *A Theory of Justice* Cambridge: Harvard University Press, 1971, p. 544.

They have taken Sun from Woman
And consoled her with Moon;
They have taken Moon from Woman
And consoled her with Seas;
They have taken Seas from Woman
And consoled her with Stars;
They have taken Stars from Woman
And consoled her with Trees;
They have taken Trees from Woman
And consoled her with Tilth;
They have taken Tilth from Woman
And consoled her with Hearth;
They have taken Hearth from Woman
And consoled her with Praise—
Goddess, the robbers' den that men inherit
They soon must quit, going their ways,
Restoring you your Sun, your Moon, your Seas,
Your Stars, your Trees, your Tilth, your Hearth—
But sparing you the indignity of Praise."

Robert Graves. *Poems 1968-1970*. New York: Doubleday, 1971. p. 48. Reprinted by permission of Collins-Knowlton-Wing, Inc. ©1968, 1969, 1970 by Robert Graves.

Contents

viii

List of Tables

List of Figures

Preface

In presenting a study of employment patterns of women in corporate America, we have tried to bring together in a coherent whole ideas from microeconomic theory and from theories of economic discrimination. The exposition falls into three parts. The first sets forth a theory of the structure of the United States economy in the context of woman's position within it; the second tests this theory in terms of its ability to explain why some firms utilize female workers more equitably than others. A theory of occupational discrimination is integrated with this test in an attempt to explain as much of these interfirm differences as possible. The role of public policy, as manifested in a number of forms, is explored as well. The last part of the book deals with public policy in historical perspective. Our findings enable us to speculate about the future of women's rights as part of the broader struggle for civil rights in American society.

Perhaps we can explain our aim in this book by reminding the reader of the long history civil rights has had as an issue in the economy. We make no claim to having isolated a new issue. We aim, rather, to apply the theoretical work recently developed by economists to an empirical analysis of employment patterns. Students of microeconomic theory often complain of its marginal relevance to issues of economic justice, because of its efficiency myopia. We find it exciting and useful in dealing with one of the many issues related to justice—the employment of women. Our hope is that this work will contribute to the literature in the economics of discrimination and in women's studies.

In writing this book we have become indebted to many people in addition to those whose work is footnoted in the text. We thank Robert T. Averitt and his wife, Brett, for continual intellectual stimulation and for reading various versions of this work. More important, we are glad that Bob's work taught us to love microeconomic theory. Cynthia Taft Morris provided invaluable econometric advice and read the entire manuscript, as well as drafts of several chapters. Her own love of innovative methodological approaches to empirical research in economic development sparked our enthusiasm for trying techniques other than the regression analyses so commonly used in the profession. Nancy S. Barrett's econometric advice was of continual help to us, as was the supportive encouragement of Charles K. Wilber. The legal insight of Betty S. Murphy was critical to Chapter 5. The American University provided essential data processing support through its Computer Science Center. The Economics Department shared essential space and materials with us. The U.S. Equal Employment Opportunity Commission, through its contract with the University for a study of affirmative action programs, sparked our interest in developing this study. The views expressed in this book are those of the authors and do not necessarily reflect the opinion or policy of either the University or of any agency of the United States Government.

Our husbands, our children, and our parents took pleasure in encouraging our efforts. We dedicate this book to them.

Women in Industry

1 Introduction

Traditionally, the dominant occupation of women in the United States has been that of homemaker. However, increasing numbers of American women are securing paid work outside the home; they are adding other occupations to that of homemaker. The focus of this book is on the nature of these paid jobs which women hold and the extent of discrimination which women face when they seek paid employment outside the home. The purpose of the book is to discover whether there are any economic, social or legal characteristics of large firms which are systematically related to the extent of occupational discrimination in these firms.

In order to discover the nature of occupational discrimination in large firms we studied the relationships among thirty characteristics of two hundred forty-six firms. Among the most important of our findings is that in the industrial sector center firms, those with the largest numbers of employees and highest asset levels, practice less occupational discrimination toward women than do smaller or peripheral firms. Among major industrial firms there appears to be a tradeoff between the share of jobs which women hold and the types of jobs in which these women are placed. One group of firms, which we call absorbing firms, use greater proportions of women, but crowd them into inferior occupations. The firms we call creaming firms employ small proportions of women but distribute women among occupations in much the same way as men are distributed. Among nonindustrial firms, those with more diversification in output and with suburban locations exhibit less occupational discrimination than do very specialized firms and firms with central city locations.

We conducted extensive interviews with male and female managers in several large firms in order to study the nature of occupational discrimination at the managerial level. One of our findings was that one problem which inhibits the entry of more women into management positions is employee resistance to female supervisors. Our examination of federal equal employment programs indicated that the federal government's civil rights enforcement efforts require additional budget and staff to make affirmative action and equal employment work effectively.

In order to set the scene for this study of occupational discrimination we will review briefly the history and current status of women in the American economy. It is important to be aware of the number of women in the labor force and the positions which they hold before examining the reasons for occupational discrimination.

1

An Overview of Woman's Role in the
American Economy

In the first decade of the twentieth century, at the same time that critics of feminism were arguing that woman's status was rooted in her economic dependence on man,[1] the number of women working for pay outside the home doubled from four million in 1890 to eight million in 1910. In 1910 females constituted a fifth of the American labor force.[2] At the turn of the century, the typical woman worker was single, young (between ten and twenty-five), and from the working class. A Senate report written in 1910 pointed out the amazing stability of sex-segregation in occupations already evident:

As a result of both machinery and division of labor, the actual occupations of women within industries do not differ so widely as do the occupations of men within the same industries. It frequently happens, indeed, that the work of a woman in one industry is almost precisely the same as that of another woman in an entirely different industry.[3]

During the present century, the largest additions to the labor force have come from married and older women. In 1947, after the end of World War II, over one third (34.8 percent) of all adult women were in the American labor force. By the sixties, half of all new entrants into the labor force were married women.[4] In April of 1972, nearly thirty-three million (32,809,000) women in America worked for pay outside their homes, representing 43.4 percent of America's female population sixteen years of age and over.[5]

A major part of the explanation of this increase in the number and proportion of working women appears to be the attempt to maintain the purchasing power of American households in the post World War II period. Instead of keeping pace with economic growth, households have found themselves struggling to make ends meet. Despite the fact that the Gross National Product grew more than 350 percent in the last three decades, per capita disposable income only doubled. The shift in the flow of funds from the household sector to the public sector has created this disparity between national growth and family purchasing power. Moreover, during this time inflation has also eroded purchasing power. The price deflator (in 1958 prices) jumped from 43.2 to 121.8 between 1939 and 1970, an increase of nearly 300 percent.

This increase in the proportion of women engaged in paid work outside the home does not appear to have been preceded by or accompanied by changes in attitudes toward working women. Additudinal research conducted in the sixties indicated that most people, including women, disapproved of women, above all mothers, working.[6] More recent research suggests that negative feelings about working women are still prevalent in America.[7]

The entrance of more women into the world of work has not yet resulted in any significant restructuring of the sex composition of occupations.[a] Women have traditionally been, and continue to be, concentrated in jobs classified as women's work. In 1960 nearly one third of employed women were in just seven occupations: secretaries, saleswomen in retail trade, general private household workers, teachers in elementary schools, bookkeepers, waitresses, and nurses. By 1970 even more than one third of working women were concentrated in these seven occupations.[8]

It should also be noted that most women are in occupations which are dominated by women. In more than half of the occupations in which more than 100,000 women were employed in 1960, at least three out of four workers were women.[9] Table 1-1 shows those occupations in which women held more than one-half of the jobs in 1970. Clearly, when an occupation begins to be thought of as women's work, men do not want to be associated with that type of work.

The work of Valerie Oppenheimer suggests that occupations in which women are concentrated share several common characteristics.[10] Although in most of these female jobs the wages are quite low, a fair amount of education is required—the average number of school years completed is higher than that of the average male worker in virtually all the occupations where women are in the majority.[11] Another common characteristic of female jobs is the need for skills or attributes that are considered female traits. For example, women are generally considered to have greater manual dexterity than men and this belief guides many employers' hiring practices. Female-typed jobs are generally those in which the requisite skills can be obtained before employment. A woman's labor force participation is frequently intermittent. An employer whose jobs require considerable on-the-job training may be reluctant to invest in the training of a woman who may leave her job. Thus the jobs for which employers are willing to hire women are those requiring skills gained through formal education prior to employment. A final characteristic common to female-typed jobs is that these jobs do not put women in supervisory positions over men. Since for a number of reasons employers and employees resist women supervisors, supervisory and executive jobs tend to be reserved for men.[12]

In addition to the sex-typing of occupations, which has resulted in a fairly definite conception of what is "proper" women's work, women are concentrated in certain occupations because they are believed to have a low

---

[a]The most comprehensive recent statistical analyses of sex-specific patterns in labor force participation are in William G. Bowen and T. Aldrich Finegan, *The Economics of Labor Force Participation*, Princeton, New Jersey: Princeton University Press, 1969. The question of why black women participate more fully than white women in the labor force is the focus of ongoing research today. Since this book is specifically about all women employed in large firms, we do not address race differences among women workers explicitly. Doing justice to that question requires another book. There is evidence that black and white women function in separate labor markets. See Larry Sawers, "Urban Poverty and Labor Force Participation: Note," *The American Economic Review*, Vol. LXII, No. 3, June, 1972.

Table 1-1
Occupations in Which Women Hold at Least 50 Percent of Total Jobs, 1970

Occupation	Number of Females Employed	Female Employment as Percent of Total Employment in Occupation	Female Employment in Occupation as Percent of Total Female Employment
Home Management Advisors	5,177	95.994%	.018%
Librarians	99,851	81.944	.345
Dieticians	36,909	91.971	.127
Registered Nurses	47,563	63.829	.164
Clinical Laboratory Technol. & Techn.	84,641	71.960	.292
Dental Hygienists	14,863	94.039	.051
Health Record Technol. & Techn.	10,283	92.108	.035
Therapy Assistants	2,118	65.960	.007
Health Technologists & Technicians	33,525	56.040	.115
Religious Workers	19,125	55.674	.068
Social Workers	135,813	62.695	.469
Teachers, Elementary & Secondary	1,674,376	70.103	5.781
Teachers, Prekindergarten & Kindergarten	122,354	97.890	.422
Teachers	106,393	70.290	.367
Dancers	4,878	82.412	.016
Demonstrators	34,462	91.039	.119
Hucksters and Peddlers	93,064	79.161	.321
Bank Tellers	214,879	86.212	.759
Billing Clerks	87,202	82.265	.301
Bookkeepers	1,255,111	81.938	4.436

Cashiers	689,461	83.722	2.436
Clerical Assistants, Social Welfare	937	78.213	.003
Counter Clerks	151,605	66.630	.535
Enumerators & Interviewers	50,091	77.578	.174
File Clerks	292,252	81.941	1.032
Bookkeeping & Billing Machine Operators	56,565	89.405	.195
Calculating Machine Operators	31,843	91.251	.110
Duplicating Machine Operators	11,526	56.876	.039
Key Punch Operators	244,674	89.765	.845
Office Machine Operators	24,553	67.827	.845
Payroll & Timekeeping Clerks	107,264	68.844	.379
Proofreaders	21,030	74.842	.072
Receptionists	287,053	94.764	1.014
Secretaries	2,638,033	97.629	9.324
Statistical Clerks	160,269	64.281	.553
Stenographers	119,875	93.150	.414
Teacher's Aides	117,359	90.272	.404
Typists	920,612	94.185	3.182
Miscellaneous Clerical Workers	302,267	63.656	1.044
Not Specified Clerical Workers	607,437	75.248	2.099
Clerical & Kindred Workers Allocated	550,108	72.648	1.901
Bookbinders	19,441	57.122	.067
Decorators & Window Dressers	40,251	57.534	.139
Clothing Ironers & Pressers	139,394	75.272	.481
Graders & Sorters, Manufacturing	24,352	64.070	.084
Produce Graders & Packers (exc. Farm)	19,356	72.958	.066
Laundry & Drycleaning Operatives	108,022	63.776	.381

Table 1-1 (cont.)

Occupation	Number of Females Employed	Female Employment as Percent of Total Employment in Occupation	Female Employment in Occupation as Percent of Total Female Employment
Meat Wrappers, Retail Trade	41,112	93.253	.142
Milliners	1,855	90.136	.006
Packers & Wrappers (exc. Meat & Prod.)	314,067	60.922	1.110
Sewers & Stitchers	812,716	93.695	2.872
Shoe-making Machine Operatives	36,419	60.213	.125
Solderers	23,851	81.615	.113
Knitters, Loopers, & Toppers	18,089	63.680	.062
Spinners, Twisters, & Winders	99,222	63.612	.342
Weavers	26,680	53.209	.092
Winding Operatives	30,939	50.937	.106
Chambermaids & Maids	186,660	94.863	.645
Cleaners & Charwomen	252,423	57.491	.872
Cooks (exc. Private Household)	523,485	63.148	1.809
Food Counter & Fountain Workers	115,563	76.339	.399
Food Service Workers	246,465	75.946	.851
Dental Assistants	86,309	97.883	.298
Health Aides (Exc. Nurses)	100,602	84.605	.347
Health Trainees	16,549	93.735	.057
Lay Midwives	537	79.555	.001
Nurse's Aides, Orderlies, & Attendants	609,022	84.825	2.105
Practical Nurses	228,648	96.421	.790
Airline Stewardesses	31,290	95.822	.108

Attendants, Personal Service	37,262	62.319	.128
Boarding & Lodging Housekeepers	5,484	71.686	.018
Child-care Workers (exc. Private Household)	122,062	93.013	.421
Hairdressers & Cosmetologists	424,873	90.104	1.486
Housekeepers (exc. Private Household)	74,265	71.861	.256
School Monitors	23,468	90.237	.081
Welfare Service Aides	11,712	76.529	.040
Crossing & Bridge Tenders	23,919	57.431	.082
Service Workers (exc. Private Household)	416,142	58.999	1.470
Private Household Workers	1,109,854	96.855	

Source: U.S. Census of Population, 1970. Prepublication tabulations. Bureau of the Census. U.S. Department of Commerce, 1972.

level of commitment to work.[b] That is, employers are unwilling to risk placing women in high status or responsible positions because they may leave or be unwilling to invest sufficient time in their jobs.

The increased concentration of women in clerical positions probably results from the fact that they are excluded from so many other occupations. Most clerical positions do not require any significant amount of on-the-job training, and rapid turnover is not as costly in this occupation as in more responsible ones. Clerical jobs have absorbed the bulk of new female entrants into the labor force between 1950 and 1970. About one fourth (26 percent) of working women over fourteen were clericals in 1950; by 1970 the concentration had increased to over a third (34.8 percent).

As the percentage of women in the work force continues to rise, this conception of women as uncommitted or secondary workers causes employers to downgrade jobs in order to fill them with less expensive female labor.[13] As examples, jobs are downgraded by taking away a part of the decision-making responsibility or status or by fulfilling certain labor requirements with part-time workers in place of full-time. Many retail firms in the economy have downgraded a large number of jobs by filling an important part of its sales force with part-time women employees. Part-time help do not get fringe benefits available to full-time employees, such as full benefits of the profit-sharing program which made Sears highly attractive to workers. The labor supply for this part-time work has come mainly from housewives who want flexible hours. Jobs filled by part-time workers tend to be viewed as impermanent and have almost no built-in protections for the worker's economic security.

Another example of downgrading of jobs comes from one of the nation's largest insurance companies. Financial officers handling mortgage loans typically have considerable individual responsibility, because they are authorized to sign off on sizeable loans. Once staffed by males, this line of work has in recent years been "turned over" to women, but at a lower position on the firm's corporate organization chart and with a narrower range of salary levels. This subtle change in employment status of women does not show up in the aggregate statistics which depict the firm's utilization of female labor. It certainly would not appear

---

[b]Randall Collins's work exemplifies the tendency to explain differences in commitment to work between men and women in America in Freudian terms. He argues that cultural forces in our society generate the self-fulfilling prophecy that women are more likely than men to have weaker motivation for achievement. He argues, unlike Tocqueville, that "A more plausible explanation is that women are the subordinate class in a system of sexual stratification. That is, there is a system of stratification by sex which is different from familiar forms of stratification by economic, political, or status group position, although it interacts with these other stratification systems. The principle of this system is that women take orders from men but do not give orders to them; hence only men can give orders to other men, and women can only give orders to other women. This principle is modified primarily when sexual stratification interacts with economic or other stratification (for example, when upper class women give orders to male servants)." Randall Collins, "A Conflict Theory of Sexual Stratification," *Social Problems*, Vol. 19, No. 1, Summer, 1971, pp. 3-21.

in the change in the share of total white-collar employment characteristic of women, nor in the female share of professional jobs. It would never be evident from a longitudinal comparison of the male and female occupational distributions. Its manifestation is the male-female earnings gap.

The sex segregation of occupations is also reflected in the small numbers of women in prestigious white-collar occupations. Approximately 15 percent of working women were in professional and technical fields and 4 percent were employed as managers in 1970, only a slight increase from 1950. By 1970 professional women remained few and far between in the most prestigious fields. Of over 56,000 architects, only 1981 were women. Fewer than 20,000 women could be found among America's 1.2 million engineers. Women held only 4.8 percent of the economy's jobs for lawyers and judges, and only 8.4 percent of those as physicians or dentists. Only 13 percent of our life and physical scientists and only 19 percent of our social scientists are women. Not quite a third (30 percent) of all writers, artists, and entertainers are women, although these fields have traditionally been more open to women than other fields.[14]

Studies of successful professional women document the fact that the multiplicity of roles as wife, mother, and professional, coupled with the widespread acceptance of the idea that a woman should sacrifice personal goals for the sake of the family, generate contradictory expectations for women at home and at work. The reactions of women professionals to these contradictory expectations seem to fall into two patterns. Some professional women with husbands and children overcompensate at work by being especially assertive and authoritarian. However, the majority of women professionals take on subservient roles at work, functioning primarily in supportive positions. For example, in law women do a great deal of the research work while men dominate the courtrooms and in architecture women do background work while on-site work and client relations are handled by men.

With respect to managerial positions, women do not hold a majority of jobs in any of the twenty-four nonfarm management and administrative occupations detailed in the 1970 Census. Women hold about 17 percent of the 36,371,000 management jobs. Most women managers are in the fields of health administration (44.6 percent of such positions), building supervision and management (40 percent), general office managers (40 percent), assessors, controllers and treasurers (38 percent), and restaurant, cafeteria, and bar managers (34 percent).[15]

In our interviews with men and women managers in major corporations, detailed in Chapter 4, we found that women managers were a much more diverse group than their male counterparts, with respect to work history and management philosophy. The route to management success in the corporate hierarchy was much more uniform for men than for women. Unfortunately, personality studies of successful women in management have been so rare that our findings are difficult to validate in light of comparable research.

In addition to the exclusion of women from professional and managerial positions, the blue-collar jobs, some of which pay well and are heavily unionized, are also off limits for women. Only 1 percent of working women pursued crafts lines of work in both 1950 and 1970. Machine operatives represented 18.7 percent of working women in 1950 but only 12 percent by 1970. Less than .5 percent of employed women were nonfarm laborers over the two-decade period.

One of the reasons for lack of female penetration into these types of occupation is that state protective laws, until very recently, limited such things as the hours women could work and the weights they could lift. (Chapter 5 discusses state protective laws in more detail.) Such limitations had especially heavy impact on women's entrance into blue-collar occupations because these are the economy's most physically demanding jobs. Another factor that appears to have restricted women's access to these jobs is that unions have been fairly successful in keeping this source of plentiful and cheap labor out of certain occupations. Approximately one fourth of all unions have no women members. Predictably, these unions represent workers doing what traditionally has been "men's work": railroads, construction, mining, firefighting.

This brief overview of woman's place in the American economy has indicated the types of positions female workers now hold. We have suggested that economic pressures, rather than any increased acceptance of women as workers, have been the major cause of this increase in the number and proportion of working women.

Unfortunately the growth of the female labor force has not been accompanied by any significant change in the sex pattern of occupations. Women are still concentrated in occupations which are viewed as "women's work." Also, women's reputation as uncommitted or secondary workers has led employers to be unwilling to entrust certain work to female employees. Women have been especially excluded from professional, managerial, and blue-collar positions in part because of these prejudices about "women's work," women's commitment, and also women's physical capacities.

Thus far we have described some of the beliefs and conditions which have resulted in occupational discrimination throughout the economy. However, the degree of occupational discrimination is not uniform in all the various parts of the economy. Some industries and some firms discriminate a great deal more than others. The goal of the statistical tests included in this book is to find some explanation for the differences in occupational discrimination among firms.

There are several theories which have been developed to explain the phenomenon of occupational discrimination. The next section reviews several of these theories. The theoretical basis of our work is different from that of these general theories in that we are interested in understanding the sources of differences in the amount of occupational discrimination among firms, rather than the general reasons for occupational discrimination.

Theories of Discrimination

Theories of discrimination developed by American economists have concerned themselves with locating the villain of the piece. Most theories current in the United States use the neoclassical theory of income distribution as the major conceptual tool. According to this theory, relative income shares are determined by the marginal productivity of the factors of production. As Euler argued, if all factors used in producing goods and services are paid according to their contribution to output at the margin, total product will be exhausted. In the simplest terms, laborers will get what they earn—nothing more and nothing less. The theory has been used as the basis for empirical studies primarily about the economic status of blacks in the American economy. The marginal productivity theory could explain why women working equivalent numbers of hours per week in similar jobs earn less than men. To explain this phenomenon with this theory, we would need only to show that women are less productive than men.

A leading example of work based on neoclassical assumptions and the marginal productivity theory of distribution is that of Gary Becker.[16] He assumes that discrimination is caused by the employer's wish to discriminate, and that the employer's "taste for discrimination" can be measured empirically. Employment discrimination, in his view, manifests itself in the hiring of whites in lieu of blacks of the same quality at the same asking wage. The result is that blacks of equal productivity at the margin earn lower wage and salary income than whites. Becker's now famous "discrimination coefficient" measures the difference between white and black wages, expressed as a percentage of the white wage. According to Becker's theory, discriminating employers are at a comparative disadvantage in hiring labor because employers who don't discriminate can hire equally productive labor at lower wages. In a perfectly competitive product market, then, the discriminating employer imposes on himself a higher unit cost of production that shifts his long-run average cost curve up so that he does not survive. The discrimination coefficient becomes a measure of the extent of monopoly power in the product markets.

Subsequent work in the economics of discrimination has tested Becker's empirical conclusions and altered his conceptual scheme. Eli Ginsberg and Elton Rayack devised alternative indexes of occupational standing that represent attempts to improve on Becker's measure of the relative economic position of blacks.[17] Finis Welch criticized Becker's conceptual scheme arguing that the "taste for discrimination" runs from employee to employee, not from employer to employee.[18]

Theories stressing the demand side date back to efforts by F.Y. Edgeworth and Joan Robinson to analyze monopsony power in labor markets. A monopsonist is an employer who buys labor power in a labor market in which he is the sole employer. Robinson's model suggested that discriminating societies may increase their income through the practice of discrimination.[19] More recently, in a similar view, Martin Bronfenbrenner defined potential monopsony as the power an employer acquires in labor markets by imposing a system of rigid rules by which workers are hired off a queue. Employers evaluate workers along the queue continuum in hierarchical order, determined by their perceived desirability. The rules for hiring adopted by the employer, and thereby determining the labor supply function, may reflect social norms, particular tastes of the employers, or other phenomena.[20] For example, they could reflect cultural norms about the occupations appropriate for men and women. Broffenbrenner's analysis, unlike Robinson's, concludes that the group discriminated against, namely blacks or women, receive payments in accordance with their marginal revenue products. The black or female labor supply function does not necessarily have to be more inelastic than the white or male supply function to be consistent with a lower wage level in equilibrium.

Edgeworth's theory of crowding in labor markets,[21] recently developed further by Barbara Bergmann, is an attempt to integrate demand with supply in explaining wage gaps between workers of different races or sexes. This theory assumes an economy producing one commodity with a constant elasticity of substitution production function utilizing capital, female (or black) labor, and male (or white) labor. If all jobs were equally open, labor would be distributed so that the marginal products of a unit of labor would be equal in all occupations. Hence, all workers would be paid according to their marginal products. The discriminatory mechanism at work in the economy results in a crowding phenomenon. Black (or female) workers are crowded into a smaller number of occupations than other workers. Their marginal products are driven down correspondingly. In this view, it is still possible for workers to be paid according to their marginal productivity, yet for sizeable wage gaps to exist on the basis of sex or race. Empirical work using several alternative assumptions about the technical relationship between inputs used in production and output shows that there would be trivial losses to whites if crowding against blacks were eliminated.[22]

Theories of human capital, developed during the last decade by American economists, have provided the conceptual underpinning for much recent empirical work on differences in wages. The theories have contributed to important research efforts aimed at determining the extent to which differences in productivity are associated with different personal characteristics and employment histories. If differences in personal characteristics such as education or experience account for observed differences in wages, then marginal productivity theory is still relevant for studying discrimination. A large part of the explanation of lower wages may reside in lower productivity due to inferior preparation for work rather than to discrimination. Lester Thurow's work serves as our example of this approach. He has estimated a human capital function in order to test the hypothesis that, in the absence of discrimination, the distribution of income would replicate the distribution of human capital.[23]

The human capital approach is especially difficult to apply to a study of women workers because there is little evidence that women receive education of inferior quality in the United States. There is, however, a fairly common belief that women's employment records are inferior because they have higher turnover and absentee rates. In fact, few firms keep sex-specific absentee or turnover statistics for long enough periods of time to verify this contention. Most studies of this question in the U.S. conclude that skill level of job, worker's age, and worker's length of service are more significant determinants of turnover than worker's sex.[24]

Jan Pen, a Dutch economist, assesses the usefulness of theories of discrimination in the following way:

The argument that women are less productive and leave their jobs at an earlier age is not always incorrect, but it does not explain the wage differential. There are social conventions, prejudices and taboos at work. They block or frustrate the chances of promotion. The other sex is crammed into lower paid jobs. . . . In all Western countries the lower rungs are overcrowded. Women are good enough to become typists or to do undemanding work in the textile industry. Where they do the same work as men, this makes the supply and demand relations in the lower regions less favourable; the disadvantages extend to men working in the same lower-paid occupations. In addition, women get lower pay. In most countries, women's wages are roughly 75% of men's; that is to say *for the same work*. If the average incomes of all women are compared with those of all men, a much greater difference is found. The discrimination is double and that considerably distorts income distribution.[25]

Kenneth Arrow has tried to build a better conceptual model of racial discrimination that can apply easily to sex. Arrow views the "discriminatory tastes" of employers as problems in perception. Employers discriminate against women because they believe them to be inferior workers. They perceive women as less career oriented, more prone to high absentee rates and turnover rates than men, and more emotionally unstable than men. Two assumptions underpin Arrow's model: employers incur personnel investment costs for hiring or firing workers, and hence have an incentive to choose a known quantity when hiring new employees; and the qualities of an individual applicant for a job are unknown to the employer beforehand. The subjective probabilities of securing a productive worker are higher for male applicants, ceteris paribus. Employers explain discriminatory acts by adopting beliefs that provide a socially acceptable justification for such conduct. Hence, the persistence of prejudice can be explained in a formal model explaining economic behavior. By prejudice, he means "a judgment about abilities made in advance of the evidence and not altered by it."[26]

A fundamental question left unanswered by these theories is, Why don't the forces of competition between men and women for desirable jobs reduce wages in the most sought-after occupations and promote ease of entry into those occupations? Dual labor markets theorists have directed their efforts to answering this question. They argue that blacks and women are concentrated in low-wage, deadend peripheral jobs partly by choice. The tradeoff, from the black or female worker's point of view, is between expensive job search procedures to pursue a long-shot vis-à-vis inexpensive search procedures to pursue an unstable job. The secondary worker settles for the easy-access job and finds herself employed, but at low wages and with no fringe benefits or job security.

The dualistic structure of labor markets reflects the dualism between center and periphery firms in the economy as a whole, according to this line of thought. A number of labor market theorists have suggested that the job structure can be reduced to two broad categories of jobs. Primary jobs are desirable from a number of viewpoints. They are the most stable forms of employment in the economy and offer many fringe benefits. They offer both horizontal and vertical mobility to the worker. Lay-off is unlikely and pension plans are good. On the other hand, secondary jobs offer few of these features to the worker. These jobs are often seasonal, temporary, or conditional. They have no career ladders attached to them and are unrelated to any pattern of skill development and advancement. They offer few if any fringe benefits. Secondary workers, the theory argues, are not helped by Keynesian economic policies designed to maintain full employment. Many secondary workers are poor, yet gainfully employed on a full-time, year-round basis. Many of them are women, as we noted earlier.

The development of the dual labor market theory prompted us to seek an explanation for the differences among firms in the extent to which they employ women and the jobs in which they place women. We will concentrate on explaining why some firms discriminate more than others rather than on explaining why all firms tend to discriminate to some extent. All firms offering stable, good primary jobs may be reluctant to use female labor in their better positions because of a belief that women are bad risks. This belief does not, however, account for differences *among* firms in their employment of women. Most studies focus on the general economic status of women in the economy. Our purpose here is, rather, to explore why all firms don't discriminate to the same degree.

Firms were selected as our basic unit of analysis because we were convinced that variations in employment patterns of women within industries are as important and as great as interindustry variations. Since many industries are becoming increasingly dominated by a small number of firms, it seemed most useful to study occupational discrimination within these large firms, rather than within the industry more generally. Further, conglomerate firms have clouded the industry/firm division, so we decided to study the discriminatory mechanisms within firms, with their interests in many industries, rather than work with industries and attempt to account for all the firms which participated to some degree in that industry. The list of firms on which this study was based is given in Table 2-2.

We wanted to test a number of hypotheses relating to interfirm differences in occupational discrimination against women. First, we wanted to test whether variations among firms in the number of their jobs which are perceived as "women's work" explains the proportion of women they hire and the jobs into which the women are placed. In other words, is the extent of occupational discrimination within a firm the result of the sex-typing of jobs? We have called this hypothesis the crowding hypothesis. Second, is any aspect of public policy related to the differences in the extent of occupational discrimination among firms? Is there any aspect of a firm's relationship with the federal government or with the public which is related to the extent of its occupational discrimination? Any insights gained in testing this relationship would be useful in suggesting changes in government policy related to equality of opportunity for women.

We were also interested in discovering if there were any systematic relationships between innovativeness of management practices, location of corporate headquarters, extent of urbanization of productive facilities, or degree of administrative autonomy of the employing unit and differences in extent of occupational discrimination among firms.

The fourth hypothesis we wish to test is whether structural variables, relating to firm size, strength, and power, explain interfirm differences in the extent of occupational discrimination against women. There are several different conceptualizations of the American economy which might have been employed in such a test.

The structure of any economy is always evolving, and the American economy is no exception. American capitalism has produced a wide variety of structures generating goods and services. The special field of industrial organization is devoted to the study of these structures and of their change over time. Microeconomic theory or the theory of relative prices has traditionally included theoretical explanations of output and prices in markets with a number of structural forms. The standard microeconomic theory text includes chapters on the purely competitive market, the monopoly or single-seller market, and markets with a few firms where entry is possible but difficult. Firms selling goods or services in markets with only a few other firms may offer products which are virtually the same as those offered by others or which are slightly differentiated products. Some attention has been given to figuring out what motivates businessmen in these four market structures. They may maximize profits or their share of the market. They may maintain some minimally acceptable profit rate while concentrating their most vigorous efforts on capturing a larger share of total sales in the market they have entered. Or, firms in some markets may be interested primarily in corporate financial autonomy and security. Profit or sales maximization would be secondary objectives for such firms.

In our work we were interested in ascertaining whether the theory that the American economy has a dualistic structure provides useful insights into the extent of interfirm differences in occupational discrimination.

The Theory of Business Dualism

The theory of business dualism grew out of theories of economic development in which dualistic structures are perceived to sharpen in the course of transition from an agricultural to an industrial economy. Recently American economists, in particular Robert Averitt, have proposed that American industry has an essentially dualistic structure.[27]

Averitt's argument is that firms in the American economy fit fairly well into a two-way classification scheme. "Center" firms are large as measured by the level of employment, total assets, and annual sales volume. They are vertically integrated and geographically dispersed with decentralized management. In contrast, "periphery" firms are relatively small, less geographically dispersed, and less oligopolistic. The typical contemporary center firm is in manufacturing. Classic examples of center firms are General Motors and U.S. Steel. Averitt argues that growth of conglomerates suggests that the center firm of the coming decades will fit this prototype. Litton and Textron are good examples of center firms of the future. Even firms in sectors of the economy which link manufacturing with the consumer, such as retailing, may be dominant enough to fit the centrism classification. Sears, Roebuck and A&P have influence over and knowledge of the technical, political, and economic forces that determine their destiny.[27] The more limited potential of periphery firms arises from their long-run cost functions, which necessarily rise beyond a relatively small level of output.

Labor economists have applied the theory of dualism to the structure of American labor markets, although they do not use the concepts of center and periphery firms. Doeringer and Piore have argued that labor markets have a dualistic structure which takes the form of a primary market as contrasted with a secondary market.[28] Piore has advanced the thesis that these markets can be distinguished by the behavioral requirements which employers in the two markets impose on members of their work forces. Primary jobs require stable employment histories of workers, while secondary jobs require instability. Most of the research supporting this thesis focuses on black workers as the source of labor supply for secondary jobs.[29] Ray Marshall has argued, however, that our economy is better described by the theory of multiple labor markets, since jobs take such a multiplicity of forms over time that a two-way classification is a gross oversimplification.[30] Dean Morse has suggested a theory of peripherality as the more realistic schema.[31] He describes the nature of peripheral jobs, and finds that these jobs are concentrated heavily in three sectors of the contemporary economy: agriculture, trade, and services. He means by peripheral those workers whose employment histories are characterized by part-time and intermittent work. These persons include the young, the old, the blacks, persons of Puerto Rican or Mexican origin, and many kinds of women. Presently, women constitute the largest number of all groups in the peripheral labor force. In contrast, the nucleus of the nonperipheral work force consists of full-time, year-round workers, most of whom are prime age white males. Morse notes that bureaucratic firms with high capital-labor ratios tend to use full-time, year-round employees. They also tend to be multiplant, multiproduct, nationwide firms. They are not, however, equivalent to center firms, as defined by Averitt.

One aspect of our hypothesis-testing which we considered extremely important was whether there was any evidence that these hypotheses were interrelated. For example, are firms with large proportions of women concentrated in traditional women's jobs dominant firms in the economy? Are firms which employ very few women those with very little innovation in their management practices?

The outline of the book is as follows: Chapter 2 contains a discussion of the research design of the study and a description of the thirty variables on which we collected data for the 246 firms in our sample. The results and interpretations of the statistical tests are contained in Chapter 3. The fourth chapter focuses on women in one particular occupational category: management. This chapter is based in part on interviews with male and female managers in major U.S. firms. The federal role in equal employment opportunity is discussed in Chapter 5. The final chapter includes some research and policy implications of our findings.

Selection of Variables and Firms

This chapter has three sections. The first describes our research design and the hypotheses we wish to test; the second discusses the variables we used to test these hypotheses; and the final section presents our sample of firms and explains the process of sample selection.

Research Design

This study of the determinants of the occupational standing of women in 246 firms posed important methodological problems related to the lack of existing theoretical work on the nature of sex discrimination in employment. In well-developed fields of scientific inquiry a theoretical model is formulated and then a particular set of data is analyzed in terms of the model. However, the theory of the determinants of the occupational standing of women has not yet been specified, so it is not possible to formulate a priori models against which a set of data might be tested. In such a situation, one procedure employed in the social sciences is to make only very general specifications of a model and to use the empirical results as a guide in the formulation of hypotheses. These hypotheses would then be tested with a different set of data. In practice this procedure involves, first, the selection of a fairly wide range of variables that appear to be associated with the phenomena being studied. Second, multivariate statistical techniques are employed in an attempt to discover the underlying regularities and patterns of interaction among the variables. Once this crude map of the basic dimensions of the subject area has been developed, more direct methods can be employed to test hypotheses and to measure the relative importance of particular variables.

Our statistical manipulations provide insights into the characteristics of firms which are associated with good performance on an index of the occupational standing of women—into the ways in which these characteristics are related to each other. That is, we are interested in determining if there are variables, such as type of output or extent of penetration of international markets, which are systematically related to our measure of occupational equality within firms.

In this study the two multivariate techniques which were most useful in determining the nature of the forces related to the occupational standing of women within business firms were the principle components technique, which is a variety of factor analysis, and the automatic interaction detection technique.

The purpose of the principle components technique is to gain insight into the nature of the underlying forces which are related to a particular phenomenon, in this case to the occupational standing of women. With the automatic interaction detection technique the object is to explain the variance of the dependent variable while taking into account the interactions among the independent variables.

Neither of the two techniques employed in this study should be viewed as substitutes for the more conventional multivariate technique of multiple regression analysis. Multiple regression analysis is an appropriate statistical technique where there is a well formulated body of theory which describes the way in which a small number of independent forces are related to the variable of interest. Given a particular set of data, hypothesized relationships can be tested empirically by means of multiple regression and the explanatory values of the independent variables can be measured. The multiple regression technique was not appropriate to this body of data because well formulated hypotheses do not yet exist.

Further, the multiple regression model assumes additivity, which means the absence of interaction among the independent variables. In the area of occupational discrimination the existence and extent of interaction among independent variables has not yet been established so the application of a technique which required the assumption of no interactions among the independent variables would have been inappropriate.

The primary purpose of principle components analysis is to indicate the structure of the phenomena underlying the explanatory variables, that is, to reduce the original number of explanatory variables to a smaller number of independent factors in terms of which the entire set of original variables can be studied and interpreted.[a] Principle components analysis is based on the assumption that the explanatory variables are to some degree systematically related to each other and the end result of principle components analysis is the discovery of the nature of these underlying relationships. This technique is helpful at the frontiers of a science where there are large numbers of variables whose interrelationships are unknown.

In the factor analytic model each explanatory variable is represented as a linear combination of underlying factors. There are two different types of underlying factors: common factors, which account for the intercorrelations among the explanatory variables, and unique factors, which account for that portion of the variance which cannot be attributed to intercorrelations with

---

[a]This section deals primarily with the usefulness of principal components analysis and the way in which it is used in this study. A detailed discussion of the principle components statistical model can be found in the following sources: Louis L. Thurstone, *Multiple Factor Analysis*, Chicago: University of Chicago Press, 1947; H.H. Harman, *Modern Factor Analysis*, Chicago: University of Chicago Press, 1960; and Irma Adelman and Cynthia Taft Morris, *Society, Politics and Economic Development; A Quantitative Approach*, Baltimore: Johns Hopkins Press, 1971, pp. 131-48.

other explanatory variables. Each variable can be viewed as a linear combination of common factors, a unique factor, and random error.

Three major characteristics of the research design are: the large number (twenty-nine) of independent variables are grouped into a small number of groups, each of which has theoretical meaning for economists; the analysis uses regression coefficients of those groups of variables which are signficantly related to the index of the occupational standing of women as the principal means of interpreting the data; a technique much like nonlinear stepwise regression analysis permits nonlinearities in the data to be studied. Our conclusions, thereby, account for nonlinear relationships because we compare our linear statistical results with results of a nonlinear analysis of the same data.

Economists, unlike psychologists and educators, have hesitated to use groups of independent variables as if they were one explanatory variable. The complaint often is that groups of variables have less theoretical clarity than single, well-chosen variables. For the purpose of applying a theory about the structure of American industry to the study of sex differences in employment, no one firm characteristic depicts the theory completely. We have no a priori grasp of the importance of a single firm characteristic among several others when it is correlated with a number of these others. The appropriate way to handle this kind of problem is to use factor analysis. Like psychologists and educators, economists may find that the resulting groupings, or factors, make little practical sense. One factor may contain variables which pertain to firm finances, other variables which pertain to firm employment, and still others which pertain to firm location. Such factors are of little help in understanding economic processes or designing policies to change them. Nor are such factors useful in designing experiments to explore the nature of a process as complex as sex discrimination. The groupings developed below used a type of factor analysis called components analysis, but not to the point of combining variables that cut across the basic theories which economists use to describe firms as buyers of labor power. We combine analytical mechanics with theoretical judgment.

The automatic interaction detection technique (AID) was originally developed to answer the question of which variables are related to the phenomenon in question, under what conditions, and through which intervening processes. The object of this technique is to explain the variance of the dependent variable while taking account of the joint effects (interactions) of the independent variables on the dependent variable. With conventional multivariate techniques such as multiple regression, the interactions among large numbers of independent variables cannot be handled easily, if at all. The theoretical importance of interaction effects should be kept in mind. A set of data may show that the overall effect of some important theoretical variable is insignificant, when in fact it is quite powerful for the relevant subgroup.

The AID technique divides the sample, through a series of binary splits, into a mutually exclusive series of subgroups. Every observation is a member of just one of these subgroups. The subgroups are chosen in such a way that at each step in the process those which provide the largest reduction in the unexplained sum of squares are selected.

Our specification of quantitative measures of firm characteristics is somewhat crude. Lacking direct measures of a number of conceptually important dimensions of firm behavior, we use indicators. We created one scale by counting the number of cases coming to trial dealing with sex-related civil rights and labor relations issues as an indicator of the incidence of these problems in firms. This measure is far less precise than the numbers engineers use to measure properties of visible objects with undeniable dimensions like density or temperature. This measure is even less precise than some traditional economic variables whose specification has gained professional agreement, such as the number of cars produced last year at a given plant.

Using variables which measure the underlying concept or dimension of behavior of interest, as well as available data permit measurement, we seek answers to these questions: Can any part of the variation in the relative occupational standing of women be associated with the centrism of firms in the economy? If so, how much? Can any part of the variation be associated with the crowding process and if so, how much? Can a part of the variation be associated with public policy toward firm behavior?

Choice of Variables

Applying the theories of business dualism and occupational crowding to the phenomenon of sex differences in employment requires the careful selection of indicators of firm behavior. Since theory is useful in simplifying complex phenomena, any theory can be misused when its application causes analytical rigidity by focusing on certain phenomena at the expense of others. Any theory, and certainly the theory of business dualism, cannot be conclusively validated in the real world, because complex processes cannot be observed directly.

Applying theory in order to generate policy prescriptions is the special challenge of economic research, and the theories of business dualism and occupational crowding contain the flexibility needed to accomplish this goal.

The implications of the theory of business dualism for the role of government are especially important in terms of employment practices subject to governmental regulation. The theory of business dualism contends that government in the American economy is much like a center firm. The federal system gives staff management functions to federal agencies, delegating line decisions to state and local units. The decentralization of administration closely parallels the management decentralization characteristic of center firms. As center firms are interested primarily in their own survival, the federal government is interested in prosperity and full employment.

This view of the role of government in the economy has direct applicability to the study of sex differences in employment.

The September 1970 reorganization of the major regulatory agency in the field of employment under the Civil Rights Act of 1964 was patterned after the pattern of administrative decentralization throughout the executive branch of the federal government. The Equal Employment Opportunity Commission, following President Nixon's directive, established regional boundaries consistent with the uniform ones for all federal programs. The decentralization of critical civil rights regulatory functions accompanied the structural reorganization. Twenty-seven district offices, aligned within ten regions of the country, acquired responsibility for all compliance activities by the end of fiscal year 1971. In its annual report to the President, the EEOC on March 30, 1972, explained the intent of the decentralization of compliance.

Under this structure, the services of EEOC are being made more readily available to the public. The staffing of regional and district offices with personnel familiar with the employment situation in the surrounding geographic area is promoting more thorough, effective and efficient case processing.[1]

For investigating charges of sex discrimination and for writing the decisions of the Commission about the merits of such charges, decentralization to the district level is a function parallel with the increasing autonomy of divisions in the economy's center firms. For individual charges, local processing will become commonplace. The strategy of the EEOC for attaining broader impact on economic inequalities between men and women at work than can be achieved through the individual charge-processing procedures is quite similar to the pattern bargaining now common between center labor and center management. In response to the EEOC petition, the Federal Communications Commission ordered public hearings on employment discrimination to which American Telephone and Telegraph was respondent. Pattern settlement of the AT&T case involved the working out of an agreement for remedy of a number of forms of sex discrimination within AT&T and its operating agencies. The EEOC, the FCC, and the AT&T units within the continental United States were parties to this agreement. This innovative procedure to civil rights enforcement began in December 1970 and appears to set the stage for continued pattern settlement through interagency cooperation at the federal level. What remains unclear is how effective this new mechanism will become. Pattern bargaining in the center economy has subsumed local to national issues, according to the dualistic interpretation of the structure of the American economy. It also poses a number of dilemmas for the American worker. Pattern bargaining takes place between center labor and center business, dealing directly with wage determination in the manufacturing sector and indirectly with all other sectors of the economy.

Wage, and then price, increases in key manufacturing industries are transferred to other sectors, with the federal government playing the role of silent partner. The dilemma faced by center labor negotiators is multifaceted. Periphery firms may fold if wages set by center labor and center management are too high. Acknowledging this possibility, organized labor has accommodated the plea of competitive periphery firms for relief from pattern wage agreements. These accommodations, made to avoid the displacement of periphery workers as firms fold, are self-defeating to big labor. Periphery workers lose faith in organized labor and the unions lose credibility with them. Nevertheless, center labor has on the whole not bemoaned the demise of periphery firms whether it has been caused by inefficiency, by failure to meet the wage pattern set by the industry, or by a combination of these factors. Another aspect of the dilemma facing labor in an economy with pattern bargaining is the migration of center firms to other economies. More than a little fear exists among center labor leaders about the displacement of American workers as firms seek less expensive labor elsewhere. National target selection and pattern settlement of civil rights problems are emerging forms of interaction between the federal government and major corporations with collective bargaining agreements reached by pattern bargaining at the industry level.

This form of interaction is potentially flexible enough to incorporate both standard policy prescriptions for reducing discrimination in employment, as reflected in theoretical models of discrimination. Many models of discrimination in labor markets conclude that eliminating differential treatment requires quantitative guidelines, such as quotas and timetables for attaining them, or subsidies to firms to create an incentive for affirmative action.[2] The approach taken by federal authorities in the AT&T case combined both policy elements. It conditioned the granting of a rate increase on the opening up of previously male lines of progression to females and of previously female lines of progression to males. The agreement by AT&T to give remedial back pay to members of the affected class of female employees who had been denied their legal rights to equality of employment opportunity was made in exchange for governmental support for its rate changes to the American consumer. This approach to public policy in the field of sex discrimination couples the design of a relief system to the design of an incentive system in one of the largest private employment institutions in the nation.

Because of the nature of the structural hypothesis we are testing, the selection of indicators as variables is not limited to influences one would expect a priori to be related directly to discrimination in employment. Instead, the indicators are taken to measure influences one expects to be related to the firm's level of economic activity and to changes in the nature of that activity in the context of the American economy. A few indicators depict characteristics of each firm's work force, which one expects a priori to be related to the occupational standing of women relative to men within the firm. The economic characteristics included depict the level and stability of firms in terms of market share, profits, assets, and the like as well as in terms of level and composition of their demand for labor. Economic process variables depict the rate of integration of firms since 1947, present locational patterns, and the technological character of the production process dominant in the firms.

Indicators of the legal status of the firm are especially interesting. One expects firms with high incidence of civil rights or labor relations litigation to perform worse than others in terms of the index of occupational standing of women. This is hypothesizing that civil rights and labor relations regulatory mechanisms work; that litigation occurs typically when the regulatory mechanisms break down. Indicators of the firm's interaction with the judicial process in other fields reflect the broader posture of the firm vis-à-vis the public interest. Several indicators are included as representatives of the sociopolitical orientation of the companies with respect to intracorporate management practices and with respect to company sales to government. The complete list of company characteristics included in the statistical tests is as follows: (1) index of the relative occupational standing of women; (2) level of assets; (3) market size (1970); (4) profit level; (5) size of work force; (6) degree of stability of assets in U.S. economy; (7) degree of stability in profit level; (8) rate of increase in demand for labor; (9) degree of stability of power in labor markets; (10) degree of vertical and horizontal integration (since 1947); (11) degree of conglomerate integration (since 1947); (12) degree of product diversification; (13) typology of center firms by predominant output; (14) predominant technology of production processes; (15) extent of penetration of international markets; (16) growth rate of earnings per share; (17) ratio of net income to equity; (18) size of white-collar work force; (19) extent of female penetration in work force; (20) extent of female penetration in white-collar work force; (21) incidence of civil rights and labor relations litigation; (22) incidence of antitrust litigation; (23) incidence of consumer protection litigation; (24) character of government demand for firm output; (25) presence of federal contract, 1970; (26) extent of participation in social programs; (27) innovativeness of management practices; (28) degree of administrative autonomy of employing unit; (29) regional location of corporate offices; (30) extent of urbanization of major facilities.

Definition of Variables

The procedures used to define indicators and to rank companies varied slightly for various company characteristics. A large group of variables come directly from published or unpublished statistics. Others are scaled from published statistics. A third group of variables are scaled from qualitative data secured from primary and secondary sources on each firm. What follows is a conceptual description of each indicator or variable and a description of classification procedures followed in developing it. The indicators selected follow the logic of the theory being tested. One group of indicators depicts the centrism or peripherality of firms, as classified in the theory which hypothesizes that the private economy has a sharply dualistic structure. A second group of indicators reflects dimensions of public policy in a number of fields, one of which is civil rights compliance itself. The third set of indicators reflects aspects of the crowding mechanism which has been hypothesized to operate in labor markets, the impact of which manifests itself in sex-typing of jobs and occupations and women and between blacks and whites.

The discussion of these three sets of indicators and of their strengths and weaknesses for measuring the behavior in which we are interested completes our conceptual scheme for studying the problem at hand. Since all three sets of indicators are relevant because of their potential for explaining differences among firms in the extent of occupational discrimination, our particular measure of occupational discrimination requires definition.

An Index of the Occupational
Standing of Women

The score on this indicator for each firm is the ratio female earnings would be of male earnings if women and men received equivalent wages and salaries within each major occupational group in 1970. The index measures the difference in male and female occupational distributions by expressing a weighted average of the female distribution as a percent of the male.[3] Let

$$\text{Index} = 100 \; \Sigma \; Y_o^m p \text{ female} \; / \; \Sigma \; Y_o^m p \text{ male}$$

Where Y_o^m = the median wage and salary income of males in the oth occupational group

       p^{female} = the percentage of all employed females who were employed in the oth occupational group in the cth company

       p^{male} is interpreted similarly.

Indexes of this kind have been used throughout the literature on racial discrimination[4] and have similar conceptual strengths and weaknesses when computed so as to compare women to men. The strength of the index is that it summarizes the pattern of employment of one group relative to another, on the assumption that wage discrimination within major occupations is nonexistent. It is a good measure of the extent of discrimination solely on the basis of unequal distributions among occupations. Its weakness, of course, is that the index will take on higher values in tight labor markets, simply because women may be the first to lose jobs in blue-collar occupations.

Legal theory developed by civil rights attorneys deals explicitly with the meaning of statistical averages, such as this index, in terms of Title VII of the

Civil Rights Act of 1964. While federal court precedents are evolving continually, substantial precedent exists at the time of this writing for distinguishing two forms of discrimination. There are specific actions directed against specific persons and there is institutionalized discrimination, often manifesting itself in customary laws and norms followed as a matter of course in the operation of internal labor markets within large corporations. According to customary law women who are ill-treated in industry have no recourse so long as the ill-treatment is not peculiar to industry. Employers can mistreat women so long as they do so in ways traditional to the community.

Most civil rights attorneys have used the business-necessity doctrine to evaluate such customary laws in order to determine whether their use constitutes a violation of the spirit of Title VII. For example, if a firm or one of its major divisions performs the task of loading freight, its employees might well be expected to lift and move heavy packages. Women may well be more adversely affected by such demands than men. The company may not exclude women as a class from employment in this line of work, although the work itself may tend to offer more opportunities for men than women. The effect of such a situation would not be viewed, per se, as discrimination and would not constitute a violation. The uniform application of work requirements in this situation has a disparate effect which is sex-specific. The general criterion for determining in such situations whether the use of a work requirement with a disproportionately negative effect on women is illegal discrimination is a straightforward one: Can the employer be held responsible for the burden of curing the deficiencies of employment opportunity for women generated by discrimination or social norms within the community? If the employer can show that it meets a genuine business necessity for his employees to possess certain skills or to acquire them as a condition of employability, the employer cannot be compelled to provide the prospective employee with the missing skill even though the employer might possibly do so without suffering serious economic injury. An appropriate remedy for women wanting jobs requiring lifting heavy weights, but not knowing how to perform the required tasks, would be initial hire under the condition that the skill be acquired.

We are interested primarily in another form of discrimination, specifically that for which the firm is legally responsible. Court precedents to date focus on both the compensation to members of protected classes for the effects of past discrimination and on the elimination of future discrimination in designing settlements in such cases. There has been general agreement that relief systems would not require the displacement of white anglo male employees in order to make room for the members of previously excluded classes in any given line of progression. Relief systems can, however, require the integration of previously female lines of progression as a mechanism for concomitantly integrating previously male lines of work.[5] The Bethlehem Steel case exemplifies a court ruling on appeal which considered wage protection necessary to the elimination of prospective discrimination. Although this case dealt with race rather than sex, the principle is equally applicable. In *Bowe v. Colgate-Palmolive*, women were given back pay based on the present earnings differential and an estimate of what their relative earnings would be but for the discrimination Colgate-Palmolive had practiced. Back pay means little, of course, to persons who win litigation under Title VII unless immediate transfer to the lines of work from which they have been previously excluded accompanies the back-pay award. If immediate transfer would require the displacement of men, the standard solution suggested by civil rights attorneys is the so-called upward red circling of the rate at which women are transferred as it becomes possible, given the business necessities of the company.

For purposes of placing our Index of Occupational Standing into appropriate perspective, the theory of remedy incorporated in the notion of upward red circling is especially interesting. Transfer at differentially favorable rates into previously all-male lines of work is justifiable in legal theory under the broader question of nondiscriminatory computation of seniority. Employers may use a number of forms of seniority in personnel policy. Either plant seniority, departmental line of progression, or occupational seniority may be the controlling form of competitive seniority in any one work unit. In work units as large as major divisions within corporations, a number of these forms of seniority may be operative. Where plant-wide seniority is operative, and where qualified women have existed in the community during the immediate past, the elimination of sex discrimination would require the same distribution of seniority for female employees as for male employees, when both groups are viewed as classes. It is likely that in many work settings in firms in this sample, the only way to generate such equality to overcome past exclusion of women is to credit women with the average seniority characteristic of men, and compute from the date of first employment in any relevant job for both groups. As is so often characteristic of employment conditions of women, occupational seniority presents serious barriers to genuine equality of opportunity. Not only must a firm open up occupations to women from which they have previously been excluded, it must credit female employees transferring into new occupations with seniority earned in previous occupations in evaluating for both promotion and layoff. Most settlements in the body of court precedent to date use the smallest possible nondiscriminatory seniority unit in making such computation, so as to avoid disrupting industrial custom.[6]

We saw in Chapter 1 that the sex segregation of occupations has been remarkably stable for several decades in the economy. The practices of both center and periphery firms regarding occupational seniority may account for a good deal of this stability. Indexes of occupational standing computed for an entire corporation will hide the variations among major divisions within the corporation, while revealing the overall effect of industrial custom with respect to entry into and seniority within occupations. Many lines of progression in both center and periphery firms represent wage rather than skill differentials. The line of progression provides employers with a system for establishing promotional opportunity for employees. An exception to this pattern is found in some units in steel and glass manufacturing, where genuinely technologically integrated lines of progression exist. Competence in performing lower-level jobs is in such situations technologically essential for one to perform competently the jobs at levels higher up the line. Occupational seniority is de facto the controlling form of seniority in technologically integrated lines of progression. Nondiscriminatory employment policies would not permit women to advance more rapidly than men in these lines, even where women as a class were excluded from entry.

Management jobs are good examples of lines of progression where technological integration and occupational seniority are irrelevant considerations. Until graduate schools of business administration became the chief recruitment source for junior executives, the route to middle management was through successful sales work. Women, the theory was, could sell only those goods directly purchased by female consumers. Their exposure to management experience was made possible primarily in the garment trades, cosmetic manufacture, and related fields. When it became clear that sales experience was not technologically integrated with management skill, large firms recruited managers who fit the style of the firm from business schools. Then the problem for women, of course, changed. They lacked graduate degrees in business administration. As our subsequent chapter on women in management points out, a number of center firms are encouraging their academic suppliers of management talent to encourage women students.

For interpreting the Index of Occupational Standing, we must keep in mind that it is not a measure of the many dimensions of firm behavior which would be relevant in determining in a legal sense whether illegal discrimination against women is occurring. The index is a rough benchmark for the year 1970 of how well one firm compares to another. A number of other dimensions of each firm's employment pattern are also relevant in establishing statistical control for some of the weaknesses in the index alone. These dimensions are captured in variables discussed below. They include the female share of total employment and the female share of total white-collar employment.

The proper interpretation of the index of occupational standing for any firm is a straightforward one. A value of 1.0 would imply that if women made what men make on the average in each major occupation, their income would equal that of men, because their distribution among occupations is equivalent. Index values for firms ranged widely in our sample, from a low of .47 to a high of 1.20.[7] One set of variables which may explain these variations in the index relate to the degree of centrality of the firms in the economy.

Indicators of Centrism of Firms

Four major indicators of the centrism of firms, according to the theory of business dualism, are the level of assets, size of markets in the domestic economy as reflected in sales level, profit level, and size of total work force in the domestic economy. Extensive assets most distinctly separate center from periphery firms. They enable wealthy firms to avert crippling losses and to outspend their more vulnerable small rivals. The maintenance of high sales volume is second in importance only to the concentration of assets for center firm survival. Through product diversification, center firms can withstand losses through one particular product for time periods long enough to force a periphery firm to fold. Attaining a maximum level of profit is less important to center firms than stabilizing a satisfactory overall profit level. Many firms in this study have maintained deficit divisions because they are important suppliers to profitable divisions or because they are useful as outlets for the output of profitable divisions.

If indicators of the level of certain dimensions of economic activity are important, indicators of the stability of these levels over the recent past are also relevant. Measures of the degree of stability of firm assets and of firm profits should be positively related to the degree of centrism of firms in the sample. Indicators of the rate of increase of the firm's demand for labor and of its stability as a powerful buyer of labor power in domestic labor markets will relate to centrism of firms unevenly. Historically, manufacturing industries have absorbed a shrinking percentage of the total work force. Center manufacturing firms, unlike center retailing, transport, or utility firms, may have less stability in their demand for labor than more peripheral concerns. The major effect of these indicators may be to distinguish among types of center firms, rather than between center and periphery enterprises.

A spectrum of eight other indicators relates to the theoretical typology of centrism-peripherality. The degree of vertical and horizontal integration characteristic of the firm is an indispensable dimension of its qualifications for the center economy. Confronted with the threat of numerous forms of crisis, corporate structures adapted first through horizontal merger, and after the 1920s and 1930s through vertical integration. Growing to a size sufficient for survival has required corporate merger, and to a lesser extent internal expansion. After the disasters of the depression, vertical integration enabled many firms to feel more secure by virtue of their ownership of suppliers and distributors.

Center manufacturing firms especially reflect the tendency to integrate in conglomerate fashion, so we include a measure of the extent of conglomerate integration. Since the late 1950s, the dramatic growth of the conglomerate business type has sharpened the interest of students of industrial structure. The acquisition of smaller firms in unrelated industries enabled center firms to buttress their corporate security from threats posed by cycles in the demand for particular product lines and by growth in the market power of factor suppliers and buyers in their traditional product lines.

A twin variable accompanying the degree of conglomerate integration is the degree of product diversification. The more center the position of the firm, especially if it is an industrial firm, the more diversified its product line is likely to be. A control for the dominant output, despite diversification, is used in the form of a typology of firms according to their predominant output. A third output-oriented indicator is especially interesting, because it reflects the technological base of the firm's mode of production. The theory of business dualism accounts for technological shifts that mold the firm's demand for labor with particular skills. Moreover, three distinctly different processes, or modes of production, depict the rhythm of American industry: unit and small batch production to customer's requirements, large batch assembly-line production, and process production of goods whose manufacture can be converted to continuous flow material. Our indicator of the predominant technology of the production process separates non-goods-producing from goods-producing firms, and further separates the goods-producing group according to these three modes of production.

Center firms, protecting themselves from the threat of increased competition from imports, have become multinational in character. Our indicator of the extent of penetration of international markets is a scale based on an estimate for each firm of the proportion of sales outside the continental United States. Little empirical work has been done to study the impact on domestic employment, especially the sex-specific impact, of the overseas expansion of center firms. Some eighty of the two hundred largest firms incorporated here have a fourth of their employees, sales, and assets outside the country.[8] Recently, the U.S. Tariff Commission estimated that overseas investment is associated with 3.3 jobs exported for every one job created here at home.[9] Organized labor, which as we have noted only peripherally represents the economic interests of women, has confronted federal officials with the prospects of weakened collective bargaining power and higher unemployment which runaway plants suggest. Some unions have organized workers in overseas plants. The United Steel Workers have helped mining unions in Surinam, while the United Auto Workers have supported locals in Ford's Peru plants. The International Union of Electrical Workers supported a strike against Bolivia's General Electric subsidiary, while also bringing an important test case of sex discrimination against GE here at home. In March 1973 the preliminary hearing began in Washington, D.C. in this interesting suit which will test the obligation of a company to give pregnant female employees the same fringe benefits other employees with temporary disabilities receive.

The two remaining indicators of centrism-peripherality are less exciting than the rest, though important conceptually. The center firm should exhibit a higher growth rate in earnings per share and in its net-income-equity ratio than the periphery firm. As Averitt so aptly puts it:

Like biological organisms their strongest instinct is to survive. They are the products of capitalism and like the system that created them, they must expand lest they contract. And by expanding their assets and diversifying their activities, they blend into the economy that contains them. So long as the general economy prospers, they prosper.[19]

Level of Assets (1970). This indicator distinguishes among firms by the level of assets employed at the firm's year-end, where depreciation and depletion are excluded from total assets. Government securities held for the purpose of offsetting tax liabilities are included. Although a number of useful indicators of economic power come to mind, assets are particularly relevant to the study of the economics of discrimination. The ability of firms to make substantial back-pay awards to women where they are the affected class in litigation under Title VII of the Civil Rights Act of 1964 depends on a number of things, but most importantly on its assets. The greater the financial resources of the firm, the less likely it is to have a genuine "business necessity" associated with keeping unit labor costs low when it violates equal-employment principles.[11] The federal courts, moreover, have used as a criterion in determining back-pay settlements the financial strength of the corporation involved, as reflected in assets. Firms are scored with respect to asset level vis-à-vis firms in the same class in an ordinal scale. Twenty-five categories were used in creating the scale.

Market Size (1970). Firms are scored according to the level of total sales to indicate the size of their markets for goods and services. The transportation and utilities firms are scored by operating revenue level, the comparable concept for firms of these types.[12]

Profit Level (1970). This indicator is the level of net income for each firm.[13]

Size of Work Force (1970). This indicator is the level of total employment in each firm.[14] It reflects the level of each firm's demand for labor.

Degree of Stability of Assets in U.S. Economy (1969-70). This indicator reflects the change in rank of each firm with respect to firms in its own class in the level of assets.[15] In this particular period, many firms abruptly cut back on spending for new plants and equipment beginning about mid-1970. The change in rank captures the net financial impact on firms, relative to firms in the same group, of both this phenomenon and inflation.

Degree of Stability in Profit Level (1969-70). Firms are scored with respect to the change in their rank among firms of the same class in terms of level of net income.[16]

Rate of Increase in Demand for Labor (1965-70). Firms are scored according to the percentage increase or decrease in total employment during this period.[17] Due to heavy layoffs in aerospace firms and their subcontractors, many firms show low or negative values with respect to this indicator.

Degree of Stability of Power in Labor Markets (1969-70). Firms are scaled ordinarily with respect to the change in their rank among firms in the same class in level of total employment. The classes of firms include industrials, retailing companies, transportation concerns, and utilities companies.[18] Twenty-five groupings of companies were used.

Degree of Vertical and Horizontal Integration (since 1947). This classification is, of course, both economic and legal. It is of interest for the present study because it indicates the effectiveness of antitrust laws, considered highly ineffective by most students of merger history. The last really important dissolution took place over sixty years ago. Firms are grouped into three categories with respect to the number of acquisitions since 1947.[19]

Degree of Conglomerate Integration (since 1947). This indicator is derived by grouping firms into three categories with respect to the number of acquisitions related to conglomerate development since 1947.[20]

Degree of Product Diversification (about 1970). This classification groups these firms, all of which are multiproduct firms, into three categories, reflecting low, moderate, and high degrees of product diversification.[21]

Typology of Firms by Predominant Output (about 1970). This classification divides firms into six groups with respect to the type of output on which the corporation is most dependent.[22]

Predominant Technology of Production Processes (about 1970). Firms are scored according to whether the bulk of their productive activity is dependent on unit and small-batch, large-batch, or process technology. Firms are grouped separately as non-goods-producing enterprises.[23]

Extent of Penetration of International Markets (1970). Firms are grouped into three categories, with respect to low, moderate, or high proportion of sales located outside the continental U.S.[24]

Growth Rate of Earnings Per Share (1965-70). This classification groups firms by the average increase or decrease in earnings per share over the five-year period. Twenty-six groupings were required to account for the relatively few firms in the sample with decreases over the period.[25]

Ratio of Net Income to Equity (1970). This indicator groups firms into twenty-five categories with respect to the value of profits, as a percentage of equity.[26]

Indicators of the Crowding Mechanism

Three aspects of each firm's employment pattern, in addition to the Index of Occupational Standing, relate to the crowding hypothesis discussed in Chapter 1. The size of the firm's white-collar work force depicts the skill requirements of the firm and establishes statistical control for one of the weaknesses in the index of occupational standing. The crowding hypothesis suggests that income differentials are best explained by an initial allocation of workers among occupations which crowd women into those jobs where their marginal productivity is low. Income differentials will reflect the extent to which this crowding phenomenon occurs. The villain, in this view, is the firm refusing to hire women in attractive jobs. An excess supply of female labor bids down their wages and leaves them no choice but to work in occupations where they have lower productivity. A measure of the skill requirements of the firm controls for the firm's demand for white collar labor in general. Of course, some crowding occurs within the white-collar ranks, as we noted in Chapter 1. Many female clericals have baccalaureate degrees and are severely underemployed, perhaps because jobs that would utilize their skills are more available to men.

To take account of this crowding process, we use indicators of the extent of female penetration in the total work force and of the extent of female penetration in the white-collar work force of these firms. If the crowding mechanism is at work among the firms in our sample, the index of occupational standing should be negatively related to both of these indicators. The prototype of the ideal firm would be one in which women hold the same share of white-collar jobs and of total jobs which they hold for the economy at large—and in which women had an index of occupational standing equal to one.

Indicators related to crowding are:

Size of White-collar Work Force (1970). Firms are scored with respect to this indicator according to the level of total white-collar employment.[27] The measure reflects the composition of the firm's demand for labor in upper-status jobs.

Extent of Female Penetration in Work Force (1970). Firm scores on this indicator are the female share of total employment (female employment as a percentage of total employment). The indicator reflects the absorption of women into the firm's work force irrespective of their placement among occupations.[28]

Extent of Female Penetration in White-collar Work Force (1970). Scores are the females' share of total white-collar employment in each firm. This indicator reflects firm absorption of women within upper-status jobs specifically.[29] Since white-collar female workers, even some of those with baccalaureate degrees, have tended to settle into clerical occupations,[30] one expects this indicator to be negatively correlated with the index of occupational standing. Firms using a lot of women in white-collar jobs, though primarily in low-paying clerical capacities, will score lower on this index than others, because the average income of all female employees will be lower.

Public Policy Indicators

These indicators of centrism and of the crowding mechanism complete the spectrum of measures selected because they enable us to test hypotheses about the structure of the economy and the way in which that structure relates to differences among firms in occupational discrimination against women. For policy analysis, six public policy indicators are critical. Both center and periphery firms interact with all levels of government. Knowing the nature of that interaction is essential if we are to suggest policy for the forthcoming decades. Three public policy variables depict the history of the firm in direct confrontation with regulatory restrictions as tested in federal courts: the incidence of civil rights or labor relations litigation; the incidence of antitrust litigation; and the incidence of consumer protection litigation. Center firms enjoy a comparative advantage over periphery firms in their ability to buy the best legal talent. Their able attorneys not only afford them litigation advantages, but enable center firms to settle embarrassing matters out of court. Center firms also can afford to employ the best lobbyists to represent their interest in the halls of government. Their ability to protect themselves from public disclosure of many dimensions of corporate behavior has been remarkable. Litigation takes place against a center firm because efforts to settle out of court fail or because federal authorities press the point.

While the judicial process is an important dimension of firm interaction with public policy, executive branch interaction is often critical to firm survival. The most important form of leverage government has on corporate behavior in the American economy is in its role as consumer. The character of government demand for the firm's predominant output is one indicator of this leverage. Another is the presence of a sizeable federal contract. As the subsequent chapter on government discusses in some detail, contract compliance was envisioned as the pivotal form of public leverage for changing employment patterns in corporate America when Executive Order 4 was issued in 1970. Presumably, firms with contracts in 1970 would perform better on the Index of Occupational Standing than firms without contracts in that year.

Our last public policy indicator tries to capture a more subtle dimension of firm interaction with public concerns. Always concerned with projecting a favorable corporate image, center and periphery firms alike employ some resources for "socially responsible" programs. Our study of the extent of participation of such programs by firms in the sample revealed a wide variety of activity related to women's rights. Activities ranged from pilot projects on day care for working mothers and fathers to job-training programs designed to place clericals in technical jobs. A number of firms in the sample have women's programs in either the corporate headquarters or in one "showpiece" division. Most firms have participated in Manpower Development programs of one kind or another relating to women.

A listing and technical description of the six public policy indicators follows.

Incidence of Civil Rights and Labor Relations Litigation (1965-70). This classification is based on the number of significant cases coming to trial in federal district courts since 1965 which dealt with labor relations or civil rights issues and in which the firm was defendant.[31] Cases are defined as "significant" when either a new issue was developing through the case or when large numbers of workers would be affected by the outcome of the case. Firms are grouped into three classifications, reflecting the number of such cases since 1965. Clearly, center firms have litigation advantages over periphery ones, primarily the resources to buy legal talent.

Incidence of Consumer Protection Litigation (1965-70). Firms are grouped into three categories and scaled ordinally with respect to the number of "significant" cases coming to trial in federal district courts since 1965 which dealt with consumer protection issues and in which the firm was defendant.[32]

Incidence of Antitrust Litigation (1965-70). This classification assigns firms to one of three scale values, depending on the number of significant cases coming to trial in federal district courts since 1965 which dealt with antitrust questions.[33]

Character of Government Demand for Firm Output (about 1970). Firms are grouped into five categories with respect to the types of goods and services they sell to the federal government. One expects that firms whose government business is in social service areas will perform better with respect to women's occupational standing than other firms.[34] The five categories are social insurance and education, natural resources and agriculture, finance, infrastructure, and defense. They are scaled in ascending order.

Presence of Federal Contract (1970). This classification follows a binary specification reflecting the presence or absence of a federal contract of $50,000 or more in fiscal year 1970.[35]

Extent of Participation in Social Programs (1965-70). This classification groups firms with respect to low, moderate, or high activity in programs with a public service component. A social service component is defined to include MDTA programs components, participation in the JOBS program, special women's programs, or the like.[36]

Other Indicators

A firm's style of management is always evolving. The pattern of evolution may explain the firm's willingness to use women in the most prestigious of jobs—those in the executive suite. Since women have held a minute percentage of total management positions at all periods in the economy's history, there is no historical reason for believing that any one philosophy about management creates a more favorable climate for women than another. However, firms with a receptivity to changes in their approach to working internally within and between divisions may also be more open to the idea of trying out women executives. Finding much wider variety than we had expected among the firms in their management practices, we developed an indicator of the innovativeness of management practices over the period 1965-70. No firm in the sample had experience with anything as foreign to American thinking as worker's management, but many have established high degrees of autonomy for units within divisions and for divisions themselves vis-à-vis corporate headquarters.

In addition to the approach to management, a set of three control variables is introduced to account for locational and functional characteristics of the firms. The regional location of corporate headquarters and the extent of urbanization of major corporate facilities may relate to firm performance on the index of occupational standing for women. Women's-rights groups have exerted most vocal pressures on the West Coast and in the Northeast, primarily in urban centers. If these pressures have had much impact to date, we expect firms with headquarters in these areas and with urban locations to perform better than others. Parent companies may perform better than subsidiaries. In the spectrum of twenty-nine indicators designed to explain the variations among firms in the index of occupational standing for women, our last four are:

Innovativeness of Management Practices (1965-70). Firms are grouped into three categories for this indicator according to the extent of innovation in management since 1965. An innovation, of course, excludes reorganizations with no accompanying change in management philosophy and practice. Decentralization, begun with increasing frequency in recent years, is classified as an innovation when change in the functional lines of authority within the corporate structure accompanies the process.[37]

Extent of Urbanization of Major Facilities (1970). This classification groups firms into four categories reflecting the degree of concentration of major facilities in urban areas within the continental United States.[38] Scaled in ascending order, major facilities may be located primarily in major cities, large urban centers with populations up to one million, towns, or suburbs and small towns.

Regional Location of Corporate Offices (1970). Firms are scored with respect to four regions based on the present location of corporate headquarters.[39] In ascending order, the regions are Northeast, West, Midwest, and Southwest-Southeast.

Degree of Administrative Autonomy of Employing Unit (1970). This classification is based on whether the employing unit is the parent company itself or a subsidiary.[40]

An Epilogue on Scaling of Indicators

An example of the detailed scaling of an indicator is in order. The predominant technology of a firm's production process is one of the more interesting indicators for this purpose, because its meaning distinguishes firms from one another with respect to the implied composition of their demand for labor. The technological base for production in the American economy falls into three distinct categories. Since some firms are service rather than goods producing, four categories were essential. The technological base implies a certain job structure to accompany the demand for labor derived from the productive activity of the firm. This does not mean that technological determinacy about job structure exists. Rather, technology is treated as one of many factors influencing the demand for labor. Unit and small-batch production centers around the particular crafts and professions whose specialization generates the particular goods desired by customers. The skill requirements of such firms are unique to the firm and production workers are typically skilled and specialized. The difference in male and female occupational distributions in these firms may reflect educational and training differences more than in other firms. Firms using large-batch production, on the other hand, tend to be price-makers and quantity takers and use unskilled production workers. In an environment where a foreman's reputation and success depend largely on his ability to fathom the mood of management, sex differences in occupational distributions are not derived from any technological mandate. They are more amenable to speedy change through management policy. Firms using process production employ skilled workers and highly educated professionals and depend on high sales volume to reduce costs. Storage of goods is virtually impossible. In these firms women are likely to break into sales jobs only if goods produced are consumed or purchased primarily by women.

Obviously, most firms in this study combine two or more production techniques. Classification is based on the technique which dominates the production of those goods most important financially to the firm. The four sets of indicators described in this chapter reflect many dimensions of firm behavior, which we hypothesize may explain the variance among firms in occupational discrimination against women.

Choice of Firms

Our sample of two-hundred and forty-six firms has been selected within the constraints of data availability to suit our purpose of using the theory of

˙Table 2-1

Scale Used to Create Indicator of Predominant Technology of Production Processes in Firms

Predominant Technology of Production Processes	Description	Scale
Unit and Small Batch	a) Production of units to customer's requirements	10
	b) Production of prototypes	
	c) Fabrication of large equipment in stages	
	d) Production of small batches to customer's orders	
Large Batch	a) Production of heavy mechanical goods	50
	b) Production of light electrical products	
Process	a) Production of any good whose manufacture can be converted to continuous material flow	90
	b) Production of liquids, gases, crystalline substances	
	c) Production of steel, aluminum and engineering parts	
Non-goods-producing Firms		130

business dualism to explain the variance in the index of female occupational standing. By no means do we account for the bulk of the American labor force in constructing the sample. Dean Morse's study of the peripheral worker in the American economy makes this point very clear.

In 1964 the five hundred largest industrial corporations (ranked by sales) in the United States employed only about 10.5 million people. When we recall that some forty-seven million individuals had full-time, full-year work experience during that year, while an additional 38 million individuals had part-year or part-time work experience, or some combination of both, it is clear that the nucleus of the work force is by no means coextensive with large-scale business organization, Averitt's center firms.[41]

In the present work we analyze the employment of women in a sample of center and periphery corporations in manufacturing, trade, transportation, and utility sectors. The complete list of the firms in the sample in Table 2-2, p. 40.

From predominantly manufacturing firms, we have selected a broad and representative sample of concerns which fit Averitt's concept of center firms. Firms engaged in raw materials processing include Kennecott Copper, American Smelting and Refining, and Phelps Dodge, three of the big four in copper.

Table 2-2
Firms in Full Sample

A.O. Smith	Burlington Industries
Abbot Laboratories	Ex-Cell-O
Acme Markets	Cannon Mills Company
Admiral Corporation	General Instrument Corporation
Aetna Life and Casualty	Chemetron
Allied Stores of New York	Carrier Air Conditioning
Allied Supermarkets	Caterpillar Tractor
Allis Chalmers Manufacturers	Ceco Corporation
Aluminum Company of America	Celanese Fibers
American Bakeries	Certain-Feed Products
American Can	Cessna Aircraft
American Chain	Charles Pfizer
American Cyanamid	Chemical Bank, New York Trust
American Enka	Chesapeake & Ohio, Baltimore & Ohio R.R.
American Felt	Chicago Bridge and Iron
American Machines and Foundry	Chicago Rock Island & Pacific Railroad
American Motors	Chrysler
American Smelting and Refining	Cities Service Oil
American Sugar	Clark Equipment
American Telephone & Telegraph	Clevite Corporation Napole
Ampex Corporation	Coca-Cola
Anheuser Busch	Colgate Palmolive
Arden Mayfair	Collins Radio
Armco Steel	Collins and Aikman
Arvin Industries	Colonial Stores
Associated Transport	Consolidated Edison of New York
AVCO New Idea Farm Equipment	Consolidated Freightways
Avon Products	Consumers Power
B.F. Goodrich Rayon Manufacturing	Container Corporation of America
Baltimore Gas & Electric	Continental Can
Bankers Trust of New York	Continental Illinois National Bank and Trust
Beech Aircraft	Corning Glass Works
Bendix	Crocker Citizens National Bank
Bethlehem Steel	Crown Corporation and Seal Company
Black and Decker Manufacturing	Crown Zellerback
Borden Foods	Cummins Engin
Braniff Airways	Cutler-Hammer
Briggs and Stratton	Dan River Mills
Brockway Glass	Del Monte
Brown Shoe Company	Dixie Quilting-Cone Mills
Brunswick	Dow Chemical

Table 2-2 (cont.)

E.R. Squibb and Sons	J.J. Newberry
Eagle-Richer Industries	John Deere Industrial Equipment
Eastern Airlines	John Hancock Mutual Life Insurance
El Paso Natural Gas	Johns Manville
Equitable Life Assurance	Joseph Schlitz Beer
Ethyl Corporation	Keebler
F.W. Woolworth	Kellogg
Fairmont Foods	Kelsey-Hayes
Federated Department Stores	Kenday Company
Fieldcrest Mills	Kimberly Clark
First National Bank of Boston	Koppers
First National Stores	Lear Siegler
Flintkote Building Products	Lever Brothers
Florida Power and Light	Levi Strauss
(Freemont Factory) H.J. Heinz Co.	Libby McNeill and Libby
G.C. Murphy	Liggett and Myers Tobacco
Gamble Skogno	Ling-Temco-Vaught
Gardner Denver	Lucky Stores
General Mills	Lykes Brothers Steamship
General Tire and Rubber	Macon Plant–Armstrong Cork Company
George A. Hormel and Company	Marshall Field
Giant Foods	Martin Marietta
Gillette Safety Razor	Mattil Inc., City of Industry
Gimbels	McDonnell Douglas
Goodyear Tire and Rubber	McGraw-Hill
Grumman Aircraft Engineering	McGraw Edison
Gulf Oil	Melville Shoe
Hanes	Mellon National Bank and Trust
Harsco	Merch and Company
Hart, Schaffner and Marx	Metropolitan Life Insurance
Haudaille Duval Wright Company	Midland-Ross
Hawmet Corporation(Air Master Division)	Minnesota Mining and Manufacturing
Hercules	Mobil Chemical Company
Hewlett-Packard	Montgomery Ward
Honeywell	Morgan Guarantee Trust of New York
Ingersoll-Rand	Motorola
Inland Steel	National Airlines
Inmont	National Bank of Detroit
International Business Machines	National Cash Register
International Minerals and Chemicals Corporation	National Distillers Products
Interstate Bakeries Corporation	National Gypsum
J.C. Penney	National Tea

Table 2-2 (cont.)

Northwest Airlines	Singer
Norton and Company	Snack Foods—Pet, Inc.
Ogden Foods	Scott Paper
Oscar Myer	Southern California Edison
Otis Elevator Company	Southern Railway
Outboard Marine	Square Deal Company
Owens-Corning Fiberglass Company	St. Louis-San Francisco Railroad
Ownes-Illinois Machine Manufacturing	St. Regis Paper Company
Pabst Brewing Company	Standard Brands Incorporated
Pacific Gas and Electric	Stauffer Chemical
Pacific Intermountain Express Company	Stokeley Van Camp
Pan American World Airways	Stop and Shop
Parke Davis	Sun Oil
Pennsylvania Central Railroad	Sunbeam Electronics
Pennsylvania Salt Chemical	Sunstrand Hudro Transmission
Phelps Dodge	Supermarkets General
Philadelphia Electric	Swift and Company
Philco Ford	Textronix
Phillips Petroleum	The Chase Manhattan Bank
Polaroid	The Detroit Edison Company
Potlatch Forests	The Grand Union Company
P.P.G. Industries, Inc. (Linseed Oil	The Great Atlantic and Pacific Tea Company
Producers)	The Magnavox Company
Procter and Gamble	The Pillsbury Company
Quaker Oats	The Southland Corporation
Radio Corporation of America	Times-Mirror Press
Railway Express	Todd Shipyards Corporation
Ralston Purina	Trane Company
Raytheon	Trans-World Airlines
Reading	Travelers Insurance
Republic Steel	U.S. Gypsum Company
Revere Copper and Brass	U.S. Metals
Res Chainbelt	U.S. Pipe and Foundry
Rockwell Manufacturing	U.S. Rubber
Rohr Corporation	Union Camp
S.S. Kresge	Union Carbine
Smith-Corona Marchand	Union Oil of California
Sears, Roebuck	United States Steel
Security Pacific National Bank	Upjohn
Shiller Globe	Valley National Bank
Sherwin Williams	Varian Associates

Table 2-2 (cont.)

Walgreen Drug	Westinghouse Air Brake Company
Wallace Murray	Westavco Corporation
Wells Fargo Bank	Weyerhaeuser
West Point-Pepperill	Wheeling-Pittsburg Steel
Western Airlines	Winn Dixie Stores
Western Electric	Xerox
Western Union Telephone	Zayre

Several members of steel's big twelve firms, which collectively account for more than 80 percent of U.S. productive capacity in steel ingots, pig iron, and finished hot-rolled steel, are included: U.S. Steel, Republic Steel, Bethlehem Steel, Armco Steel, and Inland Steel. These firms are good examples of the concept of center firms. Kennecott Copper ranked 105th with respect to sales among *Fortune*'s 1970 listing of the 500 largest corporations in the economy. Even more central as measured by level of assets, Kennecott Copper ranked fifty-seventh. It boasted nearly two billion dollars' worth of assets in 1970 ($1,737,190,000). It employed 30,500 workers. American Smelting and Refining is less dominant, having a rank of 163 with respect to sales and assets of an estimated $862,058,000. Phelps Dodge stands midway between these two in copper, with a rank of 156 according to sales and assets of $898,494,000.

Center steel firms are more powerful among industrials than center copper concerns. U.S. Steel ranks twelfth among the 500 largest industrials by sales and has over six billion dollars worth of assets ($6,311,038,000). Republic, Bethlehem, Armco, and Inland have assets ranging from 1.3 to 3.3 billion dollars.

In addition to raw materials processing, intermediate goods manufacture is a major market-orientation of manufacturing industries. Several of the center firms engaged primarily in the manufacture of intermediate goods are included in our sample. Westinghouse, one of the most dominant firms in the electrical field, is included, along with Western Electric. Westinghouse is highly diversified and decentralized. Its centrality among industrial firms is evidenced by its rank of 13 among the top 500 in 1970 according to sales volume, reflecting sales of 4.3 billion dollars. Westinghouse assets were worth 3.3 billion dollars, a level exceeded by only nineteen other firms among the 500 largest industrials. One of the three giants in farm machinery manufacturing, Allis-Chalmers, is in our sample as well. Though a center firm among farm machinery concerns, Allis-Chalmers is far less formidable an economic fortress than Westinghouse or U.S. Steel. Its sales were only .8 billion dollars in 1970, and it ranked 139 among the top 500. Its assets were .7 billion dollars. John Deere Industrial Equipment Company is a third center firm specializing in the manufacture of intermediate goods.

Three of America's leading chemical manufacturers are in the sample: Dow Chemical, Union Carbide, and American Cyanide. Two center firms providing major raw chemical materials of chemical manufacture are also in the sample: Phillips Petroleum and Eastman Kodak. Eastman Kodak, moreover, is a good example of a center firm which overlaps a number of manufacturing industry classifications. It is a leading firm in the instruments industry along with Minnesota Mining and Manufacturing. Some chemical manufacturers are especially good examples of firms coming to grips with a multiplicity of issues involved in women's rights. Hiring mostly production workers, a sizable number of whom do "trick" or shift work, chemical firms' compliance with state protective laws has meant that women do not do a number of kinds of production work, especially those where shift or "trick" work is the norm. Women have not been vigorously seeking trick work. Although federal laws supersede state protective laws with respect to hours limitations, it remains unclear whether women will take these jobs. A number of chemical firms have experimented with ways to vary the shift schedule of production workers, who until the recent past could predict five years ahead what day of the week they would be doing what particular trick. Opening up these lines of progression to women and expecting them to gear their lives to rigidly defined rotating shifts is complying with Title VII of the Civil Rights Act of 1964. Men whose lives are enmeshed in the scheduling consistent with trick work are afraid of competition from women; an intense emotion of ambivalence may characterize prospective women workers.

A third market-orientation among key manufacturing industries is government sales. Center firms specializing in goods or services for government sales include both aircraft and electronics concerns. Grumman Aircraft Engineering is one of several dominant aircraft firms, with a rank of 122 in 1970 among the top 500 industrials. Its assets were valued at $386,827,000. Center electronics firms include seven giants which collectively bring in over half a billion dollars' worth of electronics revenue annually. Four of these are in our sample: Radio Corporation of America, General Electric, IBM, and Raytheon. IBM has for some years been known as an example of a firm attempting to make real progress in the civil rights field.

A substantial number of the economy's center, or dominant, firms are in industries which specialize in consumer sales. One of the big three automobile manufacturers, Chrysler, is in our sample. Chrysler's credentials as a center firm are impeccable. It ranked seventh among the 500 largest industrials in 1970 because of its huge sales volume, $6,999,676,000. Chrysler had assets valued at a whopping $4,815,772,000.

Petroleum and rubber concerns, selling through their own or franchised outlets, have been diversifying into other industries, as have most center firms. In particular, petroleum firms have initiated operations in chemicals. Gulf Oil, Phillips Petroleum, and Cities Service Oil (now called Citgo) are center petroleum firms in our study. Two of the four dominant firms in rubber are also included: B.F. Goodrich and Goodyear Tire and Rubber. Goodyear ranked twenty-second in 1970 according to sales and listed its assets at a value of $2,955,301,000. Gulf and Phillips ranked eleventh and thirty-ninth respectively among the 500 largest industrials with respect to sales volume. They ranked fifth and twenty-third respectively with respect to assets.

As conglomerate mergers become more and more common in the economy, center firms defy industrial pigeonholing. Textron, listed Textronix, and Martin Marietta are now classic examples of the conglomerate pattern. As a conglomerate grows, it becomes more decentralized. Acquired companies continue in their own style of operation with little direction from corporate-level management. Our two sampled conglomerates qualify as center firms without question. Textron ranked sixty-sixth among the 500 largest industrials according to sales in 1970. Its assets were worth an estimated $976,085,000. Martin Marietta's centrality is somewhat less sharp, since it ranked 130 in sales. Its assets were worth $937,462,000 in 1970. This firm is of special interest in our sample because it was the defendant in the milestone case of sex discrimination under Title VII. Ida Mae Phillips charged Martin Marietta with sex discrimination because of its refusal to hire her on the grounds that she was the mother of preschool children. The firm employed, developed, and promoted males with preschool-age children and Ms. Phillips found this phenomenon puzzling. This district court disposed of *Phillips v. Martin Marietta*, 1 EOP 9906 (MD Fla. 1968), by finding no discrimination, on the argument that the work force was 75 percent female. The case now has been heard by the Supreme Court and has been remanded to the lower court, where it is awaiting further hearing.

The theory of business dualism argues that center firms are found outside the industrial sector of the economy, particularly in the trade, transport, and utility fields. Our sample includes a broad selection of center firms in these fields, especially in the field of retailing. Sears, J.C. Penney, F.W. Woolworth, Federated Department Stores, Zayre, and J.J. Newberry compose a good sample of powerful retailers in the economy. The most powerful, of course, is Sears, which ranked first among the fifty largest retailing companies in 1970. Sears sold $9,262,162,000 worth of merchandise that year. Its assets were worth $7,623,096,000.

Nine firms in our sample occupy a dominant place in the transport field, according to their rank with respect to operating revenues and assets. These nine companies include Pennsylvania Central, Trans World Airlines, Pan American Airlines, Chesapeake and Ohio Railroad, Eastern Airlines, Southern Railroad, Consolidated Freightways, Northwest Airlines, and Braniff. The airlines have been the object of considerable litigation on charges of sex discrimination under Title VII and are of particular interest for that reason. Airline stewardesses, formally classified as flight cabin attendants, have filed class action suits against a number of airline firms in an attempt to eliminate restrictions in their line of work which they have argued apply to females, but not to males. Employment criteria, such as height and weight requirements and single marital status, were applied to female flight cabin attendants, but not to males. The airline firms have fought efforts to change their staffing policies regarding stewardesses vociferously.

Utilities firms include dominant concerns, qualifying as center firms by virtue of huge operating revenues and assets. American Telephone and Telegraph, far and away the most dominant of all utilities firms, had operating revenues of $16,954,881,000 in 1970. Its assets are so extensive that no other utility is within a comparable range. AT&T had assets in 1970 valued at $49,641,509,000 while its closest rival, Consolidated Edison, reported only $4,448,918,000. AT&T is of special current interest because of the back pay settlement for women and minorities which it recently agreed to make to remedy sex and race discrimination in a number of lines of progression. In early 1973, AT&T settled in a precedent-setting administrative attempt to relate regulatory responsibilities of two different federal commissions to each other. The result was a requirement that AT&T's civil rights compliance responsibilities be met simultaneously with Federal Communications Commission agreement to grant the firm a rate increase. In addition to AT&T and Consolidated Edison, our sample contains five dominant utilities firms: Philadelphia Electric, Consumers Power, El Paso Natural Gas, Baltimore Gas and Electric, and Florida Power and Light.

Our sampling of firms includes, then, forty-nine corporations in the industrial, trade, transport, and utility fields which clearly qualify as center firms. Our qualifying criteria are asset level and sales volume, with respect to firms in the same field.

The remaining firms in the sample range from definitely peripheral to a middle ground between the peripheral and center categories reserved for peripheral firms recently acquired by center firms. Parke Davis is a good example of a recently acquired periphery firm, joining the middle ground among firms because of its new association with Warner Lambert. U.S. Rubber, a subsidiary of Uniroyal, has made Uniroyal able to diversify from various lines of rubber goods to chemicals and plastics. In the process, it has moved from periphery status to midway along the developmental process of increasing dominance. Periphery firms include firms in our sample which, despite large work forces, rank low among firms with respect to sales volume and asset level. Periphery firms also are less integrated, whether vertically, horizontally, or in the conglomerate fashion. Their degree of product diversification is much less than other firms in the study. Among industrials, Hanes, Keebler, Beech Aircraft, and Arvin Industries are peripheral. Among the top 500 industrials, they ranked among the lowest twenty firms according to sales volume in 1970. All four had less than $180,000,000 worth of sales, and less than $145,000,000 worth of assets. G.C. Murphy, Marshall Field, J.J. Newberry, and Giant Foods fall to the bottom of the set of our top fifty retailers when ranked by sales. Each of these firms sold less than $436,000,000 worth of merchandise in 1970.

This rough taxonomy of firms according to strictly economic criteria enables us to distinguish the degree of centrality of firms in manufacturing, trade, utility, and transportation sectors of the contemporary economy. We have eliminated firms employing less than one thousand full-time workers in 1970 on the grounds that they employ too few workers to shed much light on the core of the American economy with respect to the employment of women.

An application of the theory of business dualism to the woman worker requires some attention to financial institutions, especially the banking and insurance industries. Averitt argues:

The nation's major financial institutions have come to serve the center as satellites, threatened by center invasion when their prices or services are unsatisfactory—an ironic twist, considering widespread fears of a few decades ago that the captains of finance would one day be the unchallenged kings of industry.[42]

Support for this interpretation of the relationship between dominant firms and financial institutions comes from the behavior of the Dow Chemical Company, which went into the banking business in Zurich to assure its access to medium-term money and to avoid U.S. legal restrictions against ownership ties between U.S. banks and industrial corporations. Pointing out that the central purpose of the Dow Banking Corporation would be to lend financial support to Dow's European customers, John Van Stirum, Assistant Treasurer of Dow Chemical, stated in 1966:

Using chemical terminology, we visualize Dow Banking Corporation as a financial catalyst between Dow Companies, our bankers, and our customers, producing an essential raw material in scarce supply-medium term money.[43]

Since financial institutions, according to the theory, are periphery firms providing inputs for center firm use, it would be inappropriate to include the financial sector in an application of the theory of business dualism to female employment patterns. The theory argues that manufacturing, trade, transport, and utility sectors of the economy contain both center and periphery firms. Financial and service sectors are peripheral, supporting the center or core economy, and do not lend themselves to a test of whether the degree of centrality characteristic of a firm accounts for its propensity to discriminate against women. Moreover, the major characteristics of firms determining their degree of centrality are not conceptually comparable for banks or insurance firms vis-à-vis other concerns. Asset level and employment levels are comparable, but sales volume figures are not. The accounting conventions of insurance firms make the dollar value of life insurance in force in a particular year a conceptually different indicator of the firm's share of the market than sales volume of a manufacturing or retailing concern. Insurance firms deduct costs of writing new policies in the year they are written, rather than amortizing the costs over the lives of the policies. The more policies sold in a given year, the less the firm's net gain for that year will be. For any given year, the dollar value of life insurance in force reflects the face value of all policies whose premiums are currently being paid. Hence the share of insurance business going to one firm in a particular year is not reflected in the dollar value of insurance in force. Banks, on the other hand, rank their share of the market according to both the dollar value of loans outstanding and of deposits. No one figure is directly comparable to the sales for an industrial or retailing firm.

Although financial institutions are insufficiently comparable to others in this study to be included in the empirical analysis, they are critical for understanding the broad questions of economic equality between the sexes. Problems of women as employees of banks and insurance firms are perhaps less important than their problems as customers of banks and as beneficiaries of health, pension, and retirement plans managed by insurance firms whose actuaries compute benefit schedules. A good example of employment problems of women in the banking field comes from the public testimony of Bankers Trust Company of New York before the New York City Commission on Human Rights in 1970. In explaining why only 1 percent, or eight out of six hundred, bank employees earning over $25,000 a year were women, Vice-President Edward Dean testified:

What you have seen is a reflection of the fact that to reach higher level positions in the bank you have to enter training programs and learn banking in a bank over a period of years. You do not in educational institutions get prepared for the majority of positions, higher level positions, that are open in banking. So that as you look at the career structure, you are looking at people who entered the bank five years ago, ten, then fifteen, twenty, and twenty-five. And so the more senior the position you are looking at, the more you are seeing the reflection of practices fifteen or twenty years ago, and there is just no question that we had very different patterns of opportunities for women at that time, and that is the reason for it.[44]

Thus, past discrimination is the rationale for a contemporary employment profile in which women represent half of the bank's total work force, but only 1 percent of senior executive employment and only 5 percent of junior executive employment. Such arguments from companies fill the case literature of fair-employment-practices litigation, and are hardly unique to banking.

What is unique to banking, however, are the special problems women have as customers. Common banking practice, as evidenced repeatedly in these hearings, is to require female borrowers to secure a male cosigner before being given loans. Senior banking officials who have the authority to approve loans receive that authorization from loan committees whose members seldom include women. It is not customary practice to keep sex-specific statistics on defaults, so this requirement imposed on female, but not male customers, seems to reflect traditional perceptions of women as bad risks. The American Banking Association has argued that cosignatures on loans are required of male borrowers with working wives by many lenders for house and car loans.

Unique consumer issues exist in insurance as well. Health insurance programs almost uniformly do not follow the principles of equal treatment of male and female employees set forth in guidelines adopted by civil rights enforcement agencies, particularly those of the U.S. Equal Employment Opportunity Commission. Marital status, under these guidelines, is not a criterion determining the insurance benefits to females unless it also is used as a criterion determining benefits to males. Almost every group health-insurance program in industry denies maternity coverage to single pregnant women.

A single woman may pay the premiums paid by a married man with family coverage, but she has to elect to take such coverage before she becomes pregnant. Essentially, then, she must pay premiums to cover herself and any dependents she may have in the future equivalent to those paid by a man supporting a wife and children. If a single woman becomes pregnant and has not previously taken health insurance, her options for securing maternity coverage are limited. Typically she must rely on the good will of a personnel officer who will agree to apply to the adjuster for the insurance carrier for an exception in her case. The impact on health insurance rates for large group plans, such as the one the Metropolitan Life carries for General Motors, of providing maternity coverage for equivalent per person premium payment to single women has not been estimated.

In summary, empirical work designed to explain the variance among firms in the extent of occupational discrimination requires the exclusion of banks and insurance firms from the sample. Data and conceptual incomparability account for this exclusion. However, the chapter on women in management utilizes the results of interviews of both male and female executives in financial institutions.

What follows is a discussion of our research procedures and of our findings. Chapter 3 presents the results of our statistical work for the 188 industrial firms and for the 58 nonindustrial companies. After this rather extensive analysis of the determinants of the standing of women among the whole gamut of jobs in these firms' occupational structures, special attention is given to the status of women in top jobs—those jobs in management. Chapter 4 compares large to small firms with respect to their utilization of women in management and discusses differences between male and female managers with respect to management philosophy and style.

3 Occupational Discrimination in
Industrial and Non-Industrial
Firms

This chapter presents the results of statistical tests performed on the thirty
variables listed in Chapter 2. These statistical manipulations provide insights
into the characteristics of firms which are associated with good performance
on the Index of the Occupational Standing of Women—into the ways in
which these characteristics are related to each other. That is, we were
interested in determining if there are variables, such as type of output or
extent of penetration of international markets, which are systematically related to our measure of occupational equality within firms.

The analysis follows the design outlined in Chapter 2. Our hypotheses
relate several groups of variables, or indicators, to the Index. About 56
percent of the variance in the Index in our sample, occurs between major
divisions within the same firm and about 44 percent occurs between firms.
This study is not concerned about variations within firms. Its objective is to
relate the characteristics of the firms to these variations in the Index
between firms.

The first section of this chapter summarizes the major findings of the
statistical tests; the second section discusses the two statistical techniques—components analysis and automatic interaction detection analysis—which we applied; section three describes the steps in our research
procedures and the final section is a description of all of our statistical
results.

Major Findings

The results of our statistical tests suggest that the sex-typing of jobs and
centrism of firms explain a significant amount of variance in occupational
discrimination among large industrial firms. Firms with nearly equal occupational distributions for women and men are those which have only small
proportions of female sex-typed jobs in their occupational structures.
Further, the firms which are least discriminatory are the largest and most
powerful firms in the sample. Among nonindustrial firms with moderate
proportions of female employees, the best performers on the Occupational
Index are those with high degrees of product diversification, little incidence
of civil rights or labor relations litigation, suburban or small-town locations,
and contracts with nondefense government agencies. In nonindustrial firms

51

with small or large proportions of female employees, firms with little occupational discrimination appear to be those with the largest number of white-collar jobs.[a]

Statistical Techniques

The reasons for choosing the two statistical techniques employed in our work were discussed in Chapter 2. This section discusses the technical aspects of components analysis and automatic interaction detection analysis.

The primary purpose of components analysis is to indicate the structure of the phenomena underlying the explanatory variables, i.e., to reduce the original number of explanatory variables to a smaller number of independent factors in terms of which the entire set of original variables can be understood and studied. This technique is especially useful in situations, such as this one, where large numbers of variables are assumed to be related to the dependent variable and to other independent variables but the nature of the interrelationships among the independent variables is unknown.

In components analysis each explanatory variable is represented as a linear combination of underlying factors. There are two different types of underlying factors: common factors, which account for the intercorrelations among the explanatory variables, and unique factors, which account for that portion of the variance which cannot be attributed to intercorrelations with other explanatory variables. Each variable can be viewed as a linear combination of common factors, a unique factor and random error.

That is,

$$X_1 = a_{11}F_1 + \ldots a_{1m}F_m + b_1 U_1 + c_{11}E_1,$$

where X_1 is an explanatory variable, $F_1 \ldots F_m$ are common factors, U_1 is the unique factor and E_1 is the random error term. It must be kept in mind that $F_1 \ldots F_m$ represent functions of variables and not individual variables.

The mathematical principles by which each common factor is formed from the explanatory variables are as follows:

The variables that are most clearly intercorrelated are combined within a single factor; the variables allocated to a given factor are those that are most nearly independent of the variables allocated to the other factors; the factors are derived in a manner that maximizes the percentage of the total variance attributable to each successive factor (given the inclusion of the preceding

---

[a]The 246 firms in this sample are all large enough to be listed in the *Fortune* directory of major corporations. The results of the analyses may not be relevant to very small firms because discriminatory mechanisms may differ between large and small firms. However, any knowledge we can gain about these firms is especially useful, in that these companies are all major employers in the United States.

factors); the factors are derived so as to minimize the correlation between them.[1]

The a's in the equation above, the coefficients of the common factors, are referred to as "factor loadings." The factor loadings indicate the partial correlation between each factor and the explanatory variables. Each squared factor loading $(a_{ij})^2$ represents the proportion of the total unit variable of variable i which is explained by common factor j, after allowing for the contributions of the other common factors. The sum of the squared factor loadings is referred to as the communality and it indicates the proportion of total unit variance explained by all of the common factors. Typically, the sum of these squared elements is less than unity because all relevant independent dimensions of variation are not captured in the variables included in the statistical models. Communality in components analysis is analogous to the coefficient of multiple determination (R^2) in multiple regression analysis.

The results of the components analyses performed on our data are shown in Tables 3-1 and 3-2. The elements in the matrices shown in these tables are factor loadings.

In addition to indicating the weight of each common factor in explaining the observed variables, the matrix of factor loadings serves another purpose; it provides the basis for grouping the explanatory variables into common factors. Each explanatory variable is assigned to the common factor which explains the largest amount of total unit variance; i.e., the factor in which the variable has its highest loading.

Once the explanatory variables have been assigned to common factors the researcher must provide a reasonable explanation of the underlying forces which these common factors represent.

The derived variables (common factors) are of scientific interest only insofar as they represent processes or parameters that involve the fundamental concepts of the science involved.[2]

The results of the principle components analyses undertaken in the course of this research served as a basis for studying the mutual interdependence among variables which were assumed a priori to be related to the occupational standing of women and for determining the extent to which the total variance of the Index of Occupational Standing of Women was explained by each of the common factors taken separately and by the common factors taken together.

With principle components analysis it is also possible to find the value of the common factors for each observation in the sample. These values, which are called factor scores, are estimates of the values assumed by each of the common factors for each of the observations in the sample. These factor scores can be used to rank the sample observations with respect to each of the common characteristics or underlying forces. In this study the factor scores have not been included in the written material because of confidentiality agreements with firms. However, factor scores were computed for each firm in order to rank firms on that factor possessing the closest association with the Index of Occupational Standing.

A number of interesting theoretical questions challenge the user of components analysis. There is no single accepted criterion for determining the number of latent roots to extract from an intercorrelation matrix. The varimax criteria is one acceptable criterion.[3] Following this approach, one rotates components orthogonally until it appears that the maximum variation has been explained by the K estimated components. When the marginal increase in explained variance derived from an extra rotation falls below a specified number and the total variance explained by the K components converges, the varimax point is reached. Each component is a linear combination or index of variables.

A second interesting question relates to the linearity assumptions on which components analysis is based. One way to deal with nonlinearities is to criterion-scale the data base before applying a linear components statistical model. An excellent example of criterion-scaling is the work of a team of researchers headed by George W. Mayeske.[4]

The automatic interaction detection technique (AID) was also employed in analyzing the determinants of the Index of Occupational Standing. The AID results are presented in Figures 3-1 and 3-2. AID is an analysis of variance technique which takes into account the joint effects of the independent variables on the dependent variable. The AID technique is analogous to a non-linear stepwise regression analysis. In each step that independent variable is selected that accounts for the largest proportion of the overall variance of the dependent variable. However, the AID technique permits nonlinear interactions in each step of this branching process, while stepwise regression admits only linear splitting.

More specifically:

. . . at each step in the analysis, and for each candidate independent variable, all possible mutually exclusive partitions of the parent group into sub-groups, each of which includes particular (usually successive) values of the independent variable, are examined. For each possible partition of the relevant independent variable, the variance of the group means from the grand mean is calculated for the dependent variable. The "best" partition is that which maximizes the fraction of the total variance of the dependent variable accounted for by the means of the sub-groups (i.e., which maximizes the sum of the squared deviations of the sub-group means from the grand mean weighted by sample size). The proportion of parent sample variance thus "explained" by the best partition for the relevant independent variable is compared with the best partition for all other candidate independent variables. At each step in the analysis, that independent variable is selected for which the best partition accounts for the largest proportion of the overall variance of the dependent variable. The corresponding partition is then carried out, and each sub-group then treated as a new parent sample.[5]

In our study groups were candidates for splits only if they contained five observations and explained at least 5 percent of the overall variance.

The following provides a mathematical description of the automatic interaction detection technique.[6]

1. The total input sample is considered the first (and indeed only) group at the start.

2. Select that unsplit sample group, group i, which has the largest total sum of squares

$$TSS_i = \sum_{\alpha=1}^{N_i} Y^2 - \frac{\left(\sum_{\alpha=1}^{N_i} Y_\alpha \right)^2}{N_i} \tag{1.1}$$

such that for the i'th group

$$TSS_i \geqslant R \, (\, TSS_T) \text{ and } N_i \geqslant M \tag{1.2}$$

where

R is an arbitrary parameter (normally $.01 \leqslant R \leqslant .10$)

and

M is an arbitrary integer (normally $20 \leqslant S \leqslant 40$).

The requirement (1.2) is made to prevent groups with little variation in them, or small numbers of observations, or both, from being split. That group with the largest total sum of squares (around its own mean) is selected, provided that this quantity is larger than a specified fraction of the original total sum of squares (around the grand mean), and that this group contains more than some minimum number of cases (so that any further splits will be credible and have some sampling stability as well as reducing the error variance in the sample).

3. Find the division of the C_k classes of any single predictor X_k such that combining classes to form the partition p of this group i into two nonoverlapping subgroups on this basis provides the largest reduction in the unexplained sum of squares. Thus, choose a partition so as to maximize the expression

$$(n_1 \bar{y}_1^2 + n_2 \bar{y}_2^2) - N_i \bar{Y}_i = BSS_{ikp} \tag{1.3}$$

where $N_i = n_1 + n_2$

and
$$\overline{Y}_i = \frac{n_1\overline{y}_1 + n_2\overline{y}_2}{N_i}$$

for group i over all possible binary splits on all predictors, with restrictions that (1) the classes of each predictor are ordered into descending sequence, using their means as a key and (2) observations belonging to classes which are not contiguous (after sorting) are not placed together in one of the new groups to be formed. Restriction (1) may be removed, by option, for any predictor X_k.

4. For a partition p on variable k over group i to take place after the completion of step 3, it is required that

$$BSS_{ikp} \geqslant Q\ (TSS_T) \tag{1.4}$$

where Q is an arbitrary parameter in the range $.001 \leqslant Q \leqslant R$, and TSS_T is the total sum of squares for the input sample. Otherwise group i is not capable of being split; that is, no variable is "useful" in reducing the predictive error in this group. The next most promising group (TSS_j = maximum) is selected via step 2 and step 3 is then applied to it, etc.

5. If there are no more unsplit groups such that requirement (1.2) is met, or if, for those groups meeting it, requirement (1.4) is not met (i.e., there is no "useful" predictor), or if the number of currently unsplit groups exceeds a specified input parameter, the process terminates.

The first step in our AID analyses was to select from among the twenty-nine independent variables the one which accounted for the largest proportion of inter-firm variance in the Index of Occupational Standing. The split selected was that which maximized the proportion of overall variance in the Index accounted for by the sum of squared deviations of the mean value of the Index for each of the two subgroups. Thus, the firm's performance on one indicator, such as the Extent of Female Penetration of the Workforce, was used to find the two sets of firms which, on the average, had maximum variance on the Index of Occupational Standing vis-à-vis the average performance on the Index among all firms. This process isolates that variable which best groups observations with respect to performance on another variable of principal interest. It capitalizes, as it were, on nonlinearities in the relationships among variables, so as to maximize the proportion of the total sum of squares accounted for by the best sum of squares so derived. Thus, we were maximizing the variance in the Index of Occupational Standing jointly accounted for by the splitting of the observations according to this criterion.

The second splitting of the observations occurred when the variable previously treated as an independent variable became the dependent variable. Again, that independent variable which accounts for the greatest proportion of overall variance in the new dependent variable was selected. Each of the two subgroups of firms was further split into two groups, following the same criteria described above.

The ability to discover nonlinearities within a sample is particularly important in subject areas such as occupational discrimination in which the basic mechanisms of the process are not well known. Linear techniques, such as multiple regression or components analysis, cannot take account of interactions among the independent variables, but the AID technique permits such interactions or joint influences. In our work the AID results were used to test whether the components analyses were an accurate representation of the underlying relationships among the independent variables. If the variables which split the sample in AID are the same ones which have their highest factor loadings on the same factor as the Occupational Index, then the relationships among the independent variables are ones which can be interpreted from the components analysis. If the variables in AID are different from those associated with the Index in the components analysis, a good bit of nonlinearity characterizes the data base. Moreover, there would be reason to believe that there are different discriminatory mechanisms at work in different subsets of firms, and that a components analysis for the full sample could not accurately represent the differences in these two subsamples.

Steps in Research Procedures

The first phase of our statistical testing was a components analysis which included all of the two hundred forty-six firms and thirty variables.

The five factors in the resulting factor matrix explained only 13 percent of the total variance of the Index of the Occupational Standing of Women. This low percentage of variance explained might have occurred in two different ways. One possible explanation was that the twenty-nine variables which we selected were not systematically related to the Occupational Index. We rejected this explanation because the wide variety of variables touched on most behavioral characteristics of firms. The second explanation of this low percentage of variance explained was that there were subsamples of firms possessing different systematic relationships with the Occupational Index. Combining these different types of firms in a single sample had obscured the existing relationships.

There was reason to believe that the mechanisms of discrimination might be different for industrial and nonindustrial firms, so we stratified the sample on this basis. We hypothesized that since the industrial firms are goods producers, while the nonindustrials either produce services or sell finished products, the ways in which the two types of firms discriminate might be substantially different. Most industrial firms have very little contact with final consumers, while nonindustrials have a direct relationship with the final consumers.

Moreover, the industrial firms are primarily private oligopolies, while the nonindustrials are a mixture of monopolies (utility companies), government-regulated oligopolies (airlines and railroads), and private monopolistically competitive or oligopolistic firms (retail stores). The average value for the Index of Occupational Standing of Women is .88 for the 188 industrials and .93 for the 58 nonindustrials.

A number of interesting tests on the data reinforced our conclusion that the most appropriate principle or stratification in this study of differences in discrimination among firms was type of output (industrial-nonindustrial). The full sample was stratified on the basis of a number of other variables which are thought to be important explainers of occupational discrimination: level of total employment, sales level, and extent of female penetration of white-collar employment. In no case were the resulting factors any more analytically interpretable nor was the percentage of total variance explained on the Index of Occupational Standing of Women any higher than when type of output was used to subdivide the sample.

In order to test the stability of the results of the industrial and non-industrial components analyses, we undertook several types of statistical verification. First, the components analyses were repeated with communalities on the diagonals of the intercorrelation matrices. This procedure takes out the error variance. Since the communalities were fairly high, the resulting components were identical to the original ones. The stability in the composition of the components suggests that a systematic interrelationship exists. Second, in order to be certain that the results obtained in the components analyses were not sensitive to changes in the scales used on the variables, a logarithmic transformation was performed on the data. Experimental runs showed that the results of the components analysis were invariant to this transformation. A number of alternative specifications of the scaled variables also provided a basis for experimentation. Changes in specification involved changing the order of the various categories composing each scale and re-running the components analysis to test the stability of the results. The findings were not altered by such ordinal changes in scale.

Findings. Analysis of Occupational Discrimination in Industrial Firms

The components analysis for industrial firms includes observations on the entire set of thirty variables described in Chapter 2. Among the firms in this sample are automobile manufacturers, chemical and steel companies, food and beverage processors, oil companies, and electrical appliance firms. Forty-six percent of the total variance of the Index of Occupational Standing of Women is explained by the five factors shown in Table 3-1. Since most of this explanation is accounted for by Factors 1 and 2, the relationship of the Index with the other variables having their highest loadings in these factors are most relevant.

Five indicators have their highest factor loadings on Factor 1: Index of Occupational Standing of Women, Extent of Female Penetration in the Total Work Force, Extent of Female Penetration in the White-collar Work Force, Typology of Firms by Predominant Type of Output, and Extent of Penetration of International Markets.

These associations indicate that firms in which the female occupational distributions are most similar to male occupational distributions are those utilizing a relatively small number of females in the total labor force and relatively few females in white-collar occupations. In addition, more equitable occupational distributions exist in firms whose major output is in the heavy manufacturing sector and which have extensive international markets. Firms which have markedly different occupational distributions for men and women are likely to produce nondurable goods, such as textiles and processed foods, and sell very little of their output outside the United States. Large proportions of women in the work force and large proportions of women in white-collar jobs are also associated with marked differences in the distributions of jobs between men and women.

The process of occupational crowding or the sex-typing of occupations appears to be the concept that is most useful in explaining the interrelationships among the Occupational Index, the Extents of Female Penetration of the Total Work Force and the White-Collar Work Force which have their highest factor loadings on Factor 1. Sex-typing of occupations, which was discussed in Chapters 1 and 2, means that some occupations are considered appropriate for women and others are considered inappropriate. Women's work usually has the following characteristics: wages are low, but a fair amount of education is required; the jobs require attributes that are considered female traits; the jobs require skills which can be obtained before employment; and women are not put in supervisory positions over men.[7]

Juanita Kreps contends that evidence as to the segregation of the labor market by sex-typing is quite persuasive. The balkanization of much of the labor market is even given implicit sanction in our thinking: "The job classification "secretary," for example, denotes not just job skills, but female gender; nursing is so sex-typed that one must make explicit the exception by specifying 'male nurse.' "[8]

Harriet Zellner, in a recent article on discrimination against women, supports the idea that occupational segregation or crowding is one mechanism through which discrimination occurs.[9] She argues that discrimination against women in "masculine" occupations plays the central role in explaining this occupational segregation. Zellner concludes that the normal operation of the labor market is not likely to affect the relative position of women favorably, and that interference in the labor market will be required if there is to be occupational integration. The larger the share of all jobs held by female employees in a firm, the more likely it is that the women will be concentrated in traditionally female occupations. Such absorber firms have an overall demand for labor which, given

Table 3-1
Rotated Factor Matrix for the Index of Occupational Standing of Women Together with Twenty-nine Indicators of Firm Centrism, Public Policy, and the Crowding Mechanism

Economic, Legal, and Sociopolitical Indicators	(188 Industrials) 1970 Rotated Factor Loadings					h_i^2 (R²)
	F_1	F_2	F_3	F_4	F_5	
Index of Occupational Standing of Women	.57	.34	.06	.04	.01	.46
Extent of Female Penetration in Work Force	-.87	-.12	.10	.06	.07	.79
Extent of Female Penetration in White-collar Work Force	-.71	-.21	-.09	-.08	.18	.60
Typology of Firms by Predominant Output	-.56	-.14	.12	-.45	-.12	.60
Extent of Penetration of International Markets	.44	.19	.01	.21	.10	.15
Size of Work Force	.05	.65	-.15	.17	-.05	.49
Size of White-collar Work Force	-.06	.54	-.12	-.19	.16	.38
Market Size	.02	.80	.03	.07	-.07	.66
Profit Level	.05	.75	.32	.03	-.09	.69
Level of Assets	.09	.78	-.06	-.21	.20	.70
Incidence of Antitrust Litigation	.06	-.38	-.18	.05	.25	.25
Extent of Participation in Social Programs	-.09	.48	.04	.32	-.07	.35
Presence of Federal Contract	.02	.43	-.20	.07	.18	.26
Degree of Vertical and Horizontal Integration	.07	.30	-.18	.01	.06	.13
Growth Rate of Earnings Per Share	-.03	-.01	.82	-.05	.16	.70
Ratio of Net Income to Equity	-.10	.10	.84	-.10	.01	.73
Degree of Stability of Assets in U.S. Economy	-.27	.02	.37	.05	.12	.23

Degree of Stability in Profit Level	-.13	-.25	.54	-.25	.04	.43
Incidence of Civil Rights and Labor Relations Litigation	-.18	.19	-.31	.15	-.27	.26
Incidence of Consumer Protection Litigation	.12	.37	.14	-.50	-.12	.44
Character of Government Demand for Firm Output	.07	-.06	-.17	.70	.01	.53
Innovativeness of Management Practices	.13	.37	-.07	.44	.14	.37
Degree of Product Diversification	.10	.25	-.09	.48	.12	.33
Predominant Technology of Production Process	.13	.04	.07	-.65	.11	.46
Extent of Urbanization of Major Facilities	.08	-.07	.26	.51	-.16	.37
Rate of Increase in Demand for Labor	-.25	.01	.27	.18	.72	.69
Degree of Stability of Power in Labor Markets	.23	.03	.17	.17	.75	.67
Degree of Conglomerate Integration	.08	.23	-.15	.01	.56	.39
Degree of Administrative Autonomy of Employing Unit	.01	.06	-.13	.30	-.38	.26
Regional Location of Corporate Offices	-.11	-.18	-.04	.15	-.26	.14
Cumulative Variance Explained	.14	.25	.33	.39	.45	

the crowding of women into sex-labeled jobs, leads to a markedly different occupational distribution between men and women workers.

The census occupational data reveal that a great many women in white-collar occupations are concentrated in clerical jobs, and that clerical jobs are held almost exclusively by women. These facts suggest that increases in proportion of a firm's white-collar positions filled by women are associated with less equitable occupational distributions for men and women within the firm. In other words, the greater the proportion of women in white-collar occupations, the more likely it is that these white-collar women will be working in clerical positions, where there are few if any men.

The association in Factor 1 between the Occupational Index and the typology of firms by type of output is explained in part by the fact that light manufacturing firms are more likely to have female-type jobs than are heavy manufacturing firms, and thus light manufacturing firms exhibit less similar male/female occupational distributions than heavy manufacturers.

The work of R.S. Franklin on black/white economic differentials can be extended to give additional insight into the reasons for less occupational discrimination in heavy industry.[10] If employers believe that male employees would resist working with females, they may hire fewer women in occupations where the work requires a high degree of human interaction. This reluctance to hire women under certain conditions is related to employer concern that costs might increase if employee relationships on the job interfered with production. Capital-intensive modes of production (that is, heavy industry) tend to require a minimum of personal interaction; jobs may be along an assemblyline or one person may operate a single machine. Thus, an employer whose firm is engaged in capital-intensive production may be less reluctant to hire at least a few women for a wide variety of occupations than an employer whose production techniques require a considerable amount of human interaction.

The association of extent of penetration of international markets with Factor 1 suggests that those firms with extensive sales abroad are engaged in heavy manufacturing activities, rather than light manufacturing. Thus it is the type of output which probably provides the link between these internationally oriented firms and the Occupational Index. One direction future research might take is to explore more fully the impact on women workers of the behavior of multinational firms.

Census data and the variables in Factor 1 provide strong support for the hypothesis that a great many occupations are sex-typed and occupational distributions of firms reflect, in part, their share of sex-typed occupations. However, hypotheses about the way in which sex-typing of jobs or occupational crowding takes place are less easy to substantiate.

There appear to be three separate factors which explain occupational crowding. First, until the last few years state laws regulating such employment conditions as hours of work and weight-lifting limits blocked the entry of women into certain occupations. Recent court rulings have established the precedent that federal civil rights legislation supercedes state protective labor laws, so future occupational choices of women will be free of such statutory limitations. (See Chapter 5 for a discussion of state protective laws and federal civil rights legislation.) Second, cultural patterns also play a major role in sex-typing of occupations and occupational crowding. American women have not customarily considered work outside the home as an important aspect of their lives. To the extent that women prepare themselves for salaried work, they tend to choose occupations that fit most easily with the anticipated roles of wife and mother. Thus social values have resulted in the supply of women's labor being heavily concentrated in a limited number of occupations. Third, employers are in part responsible for maintaining the concentration of women in certain occupations because of their frequent reluctance or refusal to hire even qualified women for jobs which are sex-typed as male.[11] Federal civil rights actions, especially the requirement for affirmative action plans by firms with government contracts, may minimize the amount of future employer discrimination.

One way to gain additional insight into possible interpretations of factor patterns is to estimate factor scores for each observation on that factor in which the Occupational Index has its highest loading. Factor scores are estimates of the values assumed by a common factor for each of the observations (in this case, the individual firms) in the sample. These factor scores can be used to rank the sample observations with respect to a common factor. For this components analysis of industrial firms, factor scores were computed for Factor One, the factor on which the Index of Occupational Standing had its highest loading.[b]

When the firms are arrayed on the basis of factor scores from lowest to highest, the light manufacturing firms which produce such products as textiles, clothing, and processed foods are concentrated at the low end of the array. Firms with high factor scores on this component were producers of such products as steel, chemicals, and heavy machinery. This pattern of factor scores is consistent with the already stated hypothesis that occupational crowding is an important part of the explanation of firm performance on the Index of Occupational Standing. The firms with low scores are those which have as a part of their occupational mix a large number of jobs which have been typed as female jobs. The females employed in these firms tend to be concentrated in these sex-typed occupations. The heavy manufacturing firms with high scores on Factor 1 accord women a relatively small share of the jobs. However, the occupational mixes of these firms do not include a large number of female jobs, so the small numbers of women who are employed by these firms may hold a fairly wide range of positions.

---

[b]Because of confidentiality restrictions which apply to users of EEO-1 data, the names of particular firms may not be mentioned. To accommodate this restriction, we have excluded the firm names and numerical factor scores from this discussion. These data are jointly collected by the U.S. Equal Employment Opportunity Commission and the Office of Federal Contract Compliance.

Nine variables have their highest loadings in Factor 2: Size of Work Force, Size of White-collar Work Force, Market Size, Profit Level, Asset Level, Incidence of Antitrust Litigation, Extent of Participation in Social Programs, Presence of Government Contract, and Extent of Vertical and Horizontal Integration. The Index of Occupational Standing of Women has its second highest loading on this factor, which accounts for almost 12 percent of the variance of the Index. The pattern of association among these ten variables indicates that high scores on the Occupational Index (the score on the index increases as the distribution of occupations between men and women becomes more similar) are associated with firms with large labor forces and with large white-collar employment. Greater similarity of occupational distributions for men and women is also associated with large market size, high level of profits, and considerable power in the U.S. economy as measured by asset level. The configuration of variables on this factor suggests that firms with considerable comparability between male and female occupational distributions are more likely to participate in social programs, to hold government contracts, and to have undergone some vertical or horizontal integration. Finally, the occupational index is negatively related to incidence of antitrust litigation, which means that firms with fairly high degrees of occupational parity between men and women have not been involved in many antitrust suits.

A number of these variables with their highest loadings on the second Factor might be viewed as measures of the centrality of firms within the industrial sector (as defined in Chapter 2). The asset level of a firm is the distinguishing characteristic for separating center firms from periphery firms. In addition, extent of vertical and horizontal integration and size of the total work force are indicators of degree of centrality within the industrial sector. The fact that these measures of centrality have significant factor loadings along with the Occupational Index suggests that these large powerful firms perform well on the Occupational Index because they "cream" the female labor force; that is, they hire relatively few women whom they believe to be especially well-qualified but the women employees are distributed rather widely throughout the firms' occupational structures.[c]

It should be recalled that the Occupational Index does not measure the number of women employed by a firm; rather, it measures the distribution of women throughout the firm's occupational structure. For example, if a firm had ten different occupations with one hundred men and one woman in each category, its Occupational Index would be one. In a firm which operated production and administrative facilities in several locations and which produced

[c]The measures of centrism loading in Factor 2 are the major ones listed in Chapter 2. However, there are a number of other variables which we characterized as less important measures of centrism which do not load on this factor. The fact that all measures of centrism do not load together suggests that there are differences among center firms with respect to some of these variables. It is understandable, for example, that all firms which presently have high asset levels have not experienced the same degree of stability nor the same rates of increase in particular variables.

a variety of products, it would be possible to spread a relatively small number of women throughout the corporate enterprise without raising fears or objections from employees or clients. Thus, we are suggesting that part of the explanation of the relationship between the Occupational Index and the centrality of firms is that they are sufficiently large and diversified, both geographically and industrially, to hire a relatively small number of women in a variety of occupations without experiencing any resistance from employees or clients.

Note should also be taken that a large number of the firms that are powerful enough to be called center firms do not have a large number of sex-typed jobs in their employment structure. That is, their occupational structures do not contain large numbers, in relation to total employment, of the positions in which women have traditionally been concentrated. This particular type of labor demand reinforces the "creaming" character of the center firms' female employment.

The association in Factor 2 of the Occupational Index, the measures of centrality, participation in social programs, and holding a government contract suggests that center firms may also perform well on the Occupational Index because they are sensitive to social issues such as equal-employment opportunity. Their awareness of the need for equal opportunity, perhaps heightened by the knowledge of the government's interest in this effort, may have encouraged center firms to make some attempt to hire some women who could be dispersed throughout their corporate structure.

It is interesting to note that the Occupational Index and the Incidence of Civil Rights Litigation are not closely related in this components analysis. This lack of association suggests that in the industrial sector civil rights activities have not, as yet, been a significant force in opening new occupational fields for women. This lack of close association is not really surprising, because the first federal civil rights efforts on behalf of women were initiated only in 1965, and the affirmative action concept, which requires federal contractors to take steps to remedy occupational inequities, included women only in April 1972. Hopefully in the near future the occupational structures of firms will begin to reflect the federal concern for equality of occupational opportunities.

The four variables which have their highest loadings on Factor 3 depict the financial status of industrial firms. The negative association between these financial variables and the incidence of civil rights litigation may suggest that those firms which are financially the most healthy have had the power or the desire to settle their civil rights cases out of court.

The results of the automatic interaction detection analysis of industrial firms are illustrated in Figure 3-1. Of the nine variables which divided the sample in the process of binary splits, seven of the variables were included in Factors 1 and 2 in the components analysis.

The basic similarity in these two sets of variables indicates that the representation of the interrelationships among the independent variables by the components analysis is fairly accurate.

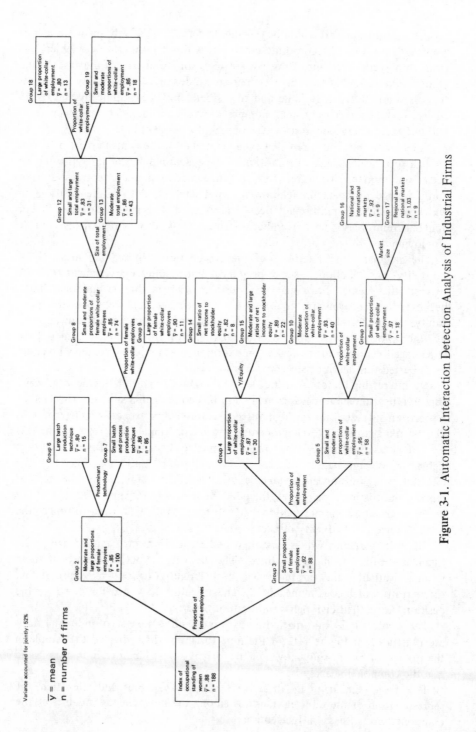

Figure 3-1. Automatic Interaction Detection Analysis of Industrial Firms

The variable which provides the best explanation of the Occupational Index in the AID analysis, the Extent of Female Penetration of the Workforce, is also the variable which has the highest loading on the most important factor in the components analysis. The power of this independent variable in explaining occupational distributions in both types of statistical tests gives strong support to our hypothesis that occupational crowding or sex-typing of jobs is one of the most important sources of occupational discrimination.

In the AID diagram Group 2 includes firms with moderately large and large proportions of female employees. Our components analysis results suggest that these firms are ones which have large numbers of "female-type" jobs into which women employees are absorbed. The firms in Group 3 employ a small proportion of women. In the interpretation of the components analysis these firms were described as ones which "creamed"; that is, they hired few women but spread them fairly widely throughout the occupational structure.

Analysis of Occupational Discrimination in Nonindustrial Firms

This components analysis for fifty-eight transport, utility, and retailing firms includes observations on the entire set of thirty variables described in Chapter 2. Forty percent of the total variance of the Index of Occupational Standing of Women is explained by the five factors shown in the rotated factor matrix in Table 3-2. The twenty-nine variables which measure characteristics of firms are not quite as powerful explainers of differences in the occupational standing among nonindustrials as they are for industrials. In the industrial analysis, 46 percent of the total variance of the Occupational Index was explained by the five factors, as compared with 40 percent in the nonindustrial case.

The clusters of variables in the five factors of the nonindustrial analysis are quite similar to the clusters in the industrial components analysis. This similarity in clustering patterns of variables means that the relationships among variables are similar for industrial and nonindustrial firms.

The most striking exception to this generalization is the factor loading of the dependent variable, the Index of Occupational Standing of Women. In the industrial analysis the Occupational Index was closely associated with factors which were interpreted as measures of occupational crowding and the centrism of firms. In this nonindustrial analysis the Occupational Index is closely associated with an entirely different set of variables; those variables which have their highest factor loadings in Factor One.[d]

---

[d]It should be pointed out that in the industrial components analysis, clusters of variables within Factors 1 and 2 could be interpreted as measures of an underlying influence. That is, a number of variables in Factor 1 were interpreted as measures of occupational crowding or sex-typing of jobs, and a number of variables in Factor 2 were interpreted as measures of centrism. In the case of the nonindustrial components analysis the cluster of variables on Factor 1 does not form an interpretable group. It appears that the variables in Factor 1 are best interpreted, in our present stage of understanding, as independent forces.

Table 3-2

Rotated Factor Matrix for the Index of Occupational Standing of Women Together With Twenty-nine Indicators of Firm Centrism, Public Policy, and the Crowding Mechanism

Economic, Legal, and Sociopolitical Indicators	(58 Nonindustrials) 1970 Rotated Factor Loadings					h_i^2 (R²)
	F_1	F_2	F_3	F_4	F_5	
Index of Occupational Standing of Women	.63	.08	.07	.03	.03	.40
Degree of Product Diversification	.59	-.14	.33	.23	-.06	.53
Extent of Urbanization of Major Facilities	.49	-.25	-.24	-.12	.31	.47
Incidence of Civil Rights Litigation	-.42	-.09	.04	-.33	.19	.33
Character of Government Demand	-.39	-.03	-.03	-.12	-.17	.20
Innovativeness of Management Practices	.14	-.33	.23	.18	-.18	.24
Rate of Increase in the Demand for Labor	-.23	-.81	-.01	-.24	.05	.76
Stability of Power in Labor Markets	.03	-.79	-.04	.11	.15	.66
Regional Location of Corporate Headquarters	.02	-.34	-.03	-.07	.01	.12
Market Size	-.12	.15	.84	.17	.13	.79
Size of Work Force	.14	-.06	.76	.31	-.17	.73
Profit Level	-.28	.28	.62	.03	.34	.66
Extent of Economic Power in U.S. Economy	-.18	-.23	.55	-.09	-.18	.43
Incidence of Consumer Protection Litigation	-.41	.23	.54	-.06	.05	.51
Extent of Participation in Social Programs	.25	.08	.39	-.18	.11	.27
Degree of Vertical and Horizontal Integration	.15	-.08	.68	.10	-.09	.50
Degree of Conglomerate Integration	.16	-.36	.52	-.07	-.50	.68

Size of White-collar Work Force	.16	.14	.12	.73	-.01	.60
Extent of Female Penetration in Work Force	.04	.05	.08	.91	.11	.86
Extent of Female Penetration in White-collar Work Force	.04	.08	.12	.87	.11	.80
Typology of Firms by Predominant Output	.59	.06	.05	.67	.16	.83
Extent of Penetration of International Markets	-.41	-.42	.06	.53	.08	.64
Predominant Technology of Production Processes	.04	-.34	-.21	.44	-.23	.41
Ratio of Net Income to Equity	.14	-.35	.25	.09	.82	.89
Growth Rate of Earnings Per Share	-.07	-.29	.22	.05	.78	.74
Incidence of Antitrust Litigation	-.11	-.32	.14	-.24	-.61	.56
Stability of Economic Power in U.S. Economy	-.06	-.03	-.10	-.01	.44	.21
Stability in Profit Level	.20	.12	-.04	-.08	.50	.32
Presence of Government Contract	-.30	.08	.31	-.23	-.45	.45
Degree of Administrative Autonomy of Units	.27	.07	.04	-.25	.38	.29
Cumulative Variance Explained	.15	.28	.37	.46	.53	

Five variables have their highest loading on Factor 1: the Index of Occupational Standing of Women, Degree of Product Diversification, Extent of Urbanization of Major Facilities, Incidence of Civil Rights and Labor Relations Litigation, and Character of Government Demand. Factor 1 explains almost 40 percent of the total variance of the Occupational Index. (This is the only factor which makes a significant contribution in explaining the variance in our dependent variable.) The combination of these variables in Factor 1 indicates that good performance on the Occupational Index is associated with moderate or high degrees of product diversification, locations in suburbs or small towns, little incidence of civil rights or labor relations litigation, and government contracts with nondefense agencies.

The association in this nonindustrial analysis between high degrees of product diversification and more similar occupational distributions for men and women may mean that as the number of products or services produced or sold expands, the variety of jobs also increases, thus permitting more women to be hired without being perceived as problems by employers or other employees. To give an example, if a store sells only one item, then its buying may be centralized, but if a store sells a wide variety of merchandise each department can have a buyer. While it may cause employee-relations problems to have a woman as the buyer for an entire store, it may not be as much of a problem if out of several buyers a few are women. The gist of this explanation is that the more segmented an operation, the easier it is for women to be spread throughout the operation and not be highly visible to other employees. Further, the more jobs there are at one level, or with one title, the less resistant the employer will be to hiring a few women into that job level.

The relationship between location of an operation and occupational parity suggests that the large supply of well-educated women in the suburbs induces employers to hire women in levels of the occupational structure other than clerical and secretarial levels. Perhaps more important, a large proportion of the nonindustrial firms are retail stores which have located in the suburbs because that is where major markets are located. In most retail establishments the majority of customers are females, who may be more willing to deal with female employees than male customers. Thus, owners and managers of retail establishments which have a predominance of female customers may be willing to hire at least a limited number of women throughout the occupational structure because it does not appear that such employees would hurt business. Thus, the association of small-town or suburban locations with more equal occupational distributions for men and women may result from a combination of supply and demand factors. These areas have a large supply of females who have sufficient education to hold positions with more status and responsibility than secretaries and clerks. Further, in these locations there is some demand for women employees to relate with female customers.

The variable entitled Incidence of Civil Rights and Labor Relations Litigation is a measure of the number of significant suits coming to trial against a firm in these areas. The factor loadings indicate that companies that have been involved in little or no litigation are the best performers on the Occupational Index. It seems too early a stage in the government's enforcement of women's equal-employment opportunity to suggest that these new regulations have yet had major effect on the occupational distributions of firms. However, the relationship between these two variables does suggest that firms that have had good employee and labor relations have been more sensitive to women's rights and have placed women in a wider variety of occupations than have firms which have had a poor labor relations record. Perhaps firms which have had little litigation are more employee-oriented; the needs and desires of the employees are an important element in the decision-making process. In such employee-oriented firms it is not surprising that the desires of women to undertake a variety of different responsibilities have been recognized and acted upon.

The fourth variable which shows a strong relationship with the Occupational Index is Character of Government Demand. The association of these two variables in Factor 1 indicates that the nonindustrial firms which have government contracts with nondefense agencies have better occupational distributions than do firms which hold contracts with defense-related agencies.

Since all the firms in this sub-sample are non-industrial firms, the goods and services they are selling to government agencies—power, transportation services, etc. cannot be distinguished as defense or non-defense goods and services. That is, none of these firms are supplying tanks or airplanes or any other product which might easily be identified as defense related. Any assumption that the nature of the goods purchased from these firms is related to the Occupational Index appears unwarranted. What does seem clear is that in those government agencies which award the major share of government contracts (the defense agencies), the contractor firms are not performing well in the area of occupational equality.

Because affirmative action programs for women are a very new feature of the government's contract compliance effort (firms were required to develop these plans only in 1971), these factor loadings cannot be construed as a lack of enforcement on the part of defense-related agencies. These factor loadings should serve as warnings to the defense-related government agencies that the nonindustrial firms with which they have had dealings are poor performers in the area of occupational equality and aggressive enforcement will be required if these companies are to be brought into compliance on affirmative action plans.

Factor scores were computed for the fifty-eight nonindustrial firms on Factor 1; the factor on which the Index of the Occupational Standing of Women had its highest loading. The firms which had the highest factor scores on Factor 1 were almost all retail stores; grocery store chains and general merchandise chains. These firms have large numbers of suburban and small-town locations. Further, these stores sell a wide variety of goods and services and have a great many different kinds of jobs in their occupational structures.

An automatic interaction detection analysis was run for nonindustrial firms; the results are illustrated in Figure 3-2. The variable which best explains the Occupational Index in the AID analysis is the Extent of Female Penetration of the Work Force. The fact that the latter variable is not closely associated with the Index in the components analysis indicates that there are some nonlinear relationships among the variables in this nonindustrial sample. It appears that among the nonindustrial firms there are different types of discriminatory mechanisms which operate within two groups of nonindustrials: those firms which are either creamers or absorbers of women and those which give women about an average share of all jobs. The components analysis technique does not distinguish differences of this type; it simply presents an average measure of interrelationships among the independent variables. The AID technique can identify systematic differences within a set of observations and has done so in this nonindustrial set.

The Extent of Female Penetration of the Work Force is the same variable which provided the best explanation of the Index in the industrial sample. The similarity of AID results among the industrial and nonindustrial samples in this regard suggests that for large U.S. firms the variable which is most important in explaining the occupational distribution of women within a firm is the proportion of female employees. In the industrial sample we suggested that firms with large proportions of female employees have considerable occupational discrimination because they have large numbers of female sex-typed jobs which they fill with female workers. However, in this nonindustrial sample the split on proportion of female employees is not between firms with large and small proportions. The AID results in Figure 3-2 indicate that firms with moderate proportions of women (Group 2) have different discriminatory mechanisms than firms with either large or small proportions of women (Group 3). The difference between the industrials and nonindustrials in the way this variable splits indicates that the factors associated with discrimination are different for the two types of firms. For the nonindustrials, in firms with fairly large or small proportions of female employees (Group 3) the proportion of white-collar positions in the firm and management innovation are the important explanatory variables, while in firms with moderate proportions of women (Group 2) a different set of forces, including product diversification and urbanization, may explain occupational discrimination. These latter two variables were closely related with the Occupational Index in the components analysis. It appears that the firms in Group 2 dominated the results of the components analysis.

Combining the components analysis and AID results, we can say that among large nonindustrial firms with moderate proportions of female employees, more equitable occupational distributions are associated with suburban and small-town locations, high degrees of product diversification, and probably with little incidence of civil rights or labor relations litigation and government contracts with nondefense agencies. Among nonindustrials with small or large proportions

73

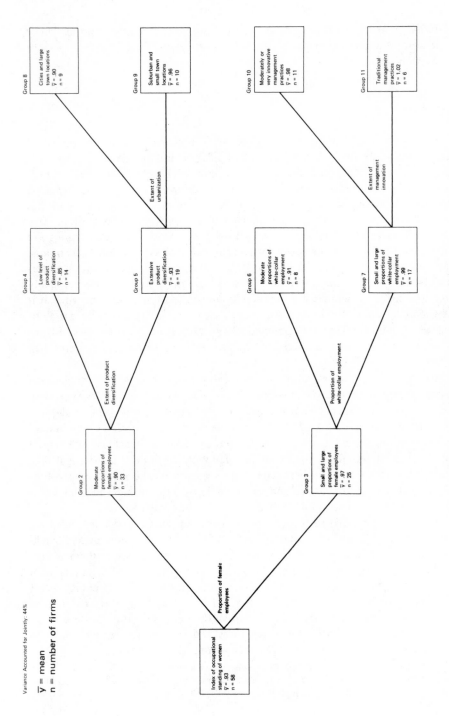

Variance Accounted for Jointly: 44%

$\bar{y}$ = mean
n = number of firms

Group 8
Cities and large
town locations
$\bar{y}$ = .90
n = 9

Group 9
Suburban and
small town
locations
$\bar{y}$ = .96
n = 10

Group 10
Moderately or
very innovative
management
practices
$\bar{y}$ = .98
n = 11

Group 11
Traditional
management
practices
$\bar{y}$ = 1.02
n = 6

Group 4
Low level of
product
diversification
$\bar{y}$ = .85
n = 14

Group 5
Extensive
product
diversification
$\bar{y}$ = .93
n = 19

Group 6
Moderate
proportions of
white-collar
employment
$\bar{y}$ = .91
n = 8

Group 7
Small and large
proportions of
white-collar
employment
$\bar{y}$ = .99
n = 17

Extent of
urbanization

Extent of
management
innovation

Group 2
Moderate
proportions of
female employees
$\bar{y}$ = .90
n = 33

Group 3
Small and large
proportions of
female employees
$\bar{y}$ = .97
n = 25

Extent of product
diversification

Proportion of
white-collar employment

Proportion of female
employees

Index of occupational
standing of women
$\bar{y}$ = .93
n = 58

Figure 3-2. Automatic Interaction Detection Analysis of Nonindustrial Firms

of female employees the degree of occupational discrimination appears to be related to the proportion of white-collar jobs within firms and management innovation.

Summary

Chapter 1 provided a discussion of some leading theories of the causes of discrimination in the U.S. economy. Many of these theories describe the factors associated with sex discrimination on a macroeconomic level; that is, they explain why the general phenomenon of sex discrimination exists. Prevailing attitudes about women workers are a phenomenon of this type. Our work has been an attempt to go beyond the analysis of the general sources of discrimination to discover the reasons that some firms discriminate more than others. We narrowed the focus of our work by concentrating on occupational discrimination because existing evidence indicates that occupational discrimination underlies a great deal of wage discrimination. While there are still a great many situations in which women are paid less than men for doing the same work, it is even more common for women to be unable to gain access to a wide variety of jobs which men fill. We have examined a large number of characteristics of firms in order to determine the reasons that some firms discriminate more than others.[e]

Among the industrial firms in our sample the degree of occupational discrimination is related to the proportion of jobs that are female sex-typed and the centrality of firms. Firms engaged in light manufacturing and food processing have large numbers of female sex-typed jobs and the large numbers of women within these firms are concentrated in these occupations. The largest industrial firms employ women more widely throughout their occupational structure, perhaps because these firms have so many locations and subdivisions and a small proportion of women can hold fairly responsible and high status positions without threatening either their superiors or coworkers.

Among nonindustrial firms, good performance on the Occupational Index for firms with moderate proportions of women is related to suburban and small-town location of facilities, high degree of product diversification, little incidence of civil rights and labor relations litigation, and government contracts with nondefense agencies. For nonindustrials with large or small proportions of female employees the occupational distribution of women is related to the proportion of white-collar jobs in the firms and to management innovation.

Our work in formulating the Occupational Index confirms the fact that there are significant interfirm differences in occupational discrimination.

---

[e]Gary Becker, in *The Economics of Discrimination*, Chicago: The University of Chicago Press, 1971, argues that competitive firms discriminate less than monopolistic firms. Since none of our firms could be categorized as competitive, we are not able to test this hypothesis.

More particularly, some answers to the questions posed at the beginning of this chapter emerge. The crowding process accounts for a significant portion of the variance in the relative occupational standing of women among industrial firms. The degree of centrism these firms enjoy within the dualistic structure of the economy's industrial sector also accounts for a significant portion of the variance. Public policy has a lesser impact among these firms. The only significant public policy indicator is the extent of firm participation in social programs. That this indicator was significant is a sign of hope. Center firms, ever concerned about public image, are more responsive to pressures from interest groups and from government. Our finding that women have higher indexes of occupational standing in firms which participate most fully in relevant social programs evidences this response.

Among nonindustrial firms, the theory of business dualism breaks down as an interpretation of the structure of the economy which helps explain occupational discrimination. The centrism of firms is not significant in accounting for the variance in the Index. The crowding hypothesis breaks down as well, with a slight qualification. The indicators of crowding cluster together but are not significantly related to the Index of Occupational Standing in the components analysis. Yet the extent of female penetration of the firm's total work force provided the best partition of the fifty-eight nonindustrial firms with respect to the Index. The components results cannot be used to reject the crowding hypothesis for utility, transport, and retail firms. The AID results show that the fifty-eight firms are best subdivided into the absorbers and creamers of female labor on the one hand and the average users of female labor on the other. Once divided, the indicators of product diversification and urbanization further divide the average user firms. We believe that the average users dominated the components analysis—this tradeoff between the female share of jobs and their relative occupational standing is not striking when all fifty-eight firms are analyzed together.

Although firm centrism and the crowding process do not appear relevant to explaining differences in the extent of occupational discrimination among nonindustrial firms, public policy does. That firms with little incidence of civil rights or labor relations litigation perform better on the Index of Occupational Standing is encouraging. It suggests that the federal regulatory and judicial mechanism works in these sectors of the economy. Litigation, as the crafters of the Civil Rights Act had hoped, involves the poorest performers among these firms. Since 1964, when sex discrimination became illegal in private employment under Title VII, both women and men have filed charges of sex discrimination against their employers. Many of these charges are without legal merit and the Equal Employment Opportunity Commission does not find cause to believe that discrimination took place. Many of those charges which generate a finding of cause are dropped because the firm agrees to conciliate. Others are simply abandoned by their initiators because they tire of the problem and decide not to cause trouble. Those cases which actually come to trial are those over which the charging parties are very angry indeed. Our results suggest that they are angry most often because their employer has a poorer employment pattern for women than other firms in the same sector.

There appear to be a number of remedies to female sex-typing of occupations. Since sex-typing of jobs is based in part on societal conceptions of "appropriate" work for women, social prejudices will have to be eliminated before women can have free access to the full range of occupations in this economy. The elimination of bias against women entering certain occupations means that young women will be encouraged to train for a wider range of occupations, and that trained women will not be rejected when they apply for particular positions.

The relationship between centrism and occupational equality seems to be the basis for optimism. Average firm size has been increasing, especially as a result of various types of merger. If larger firms (in terms of assets) discriminate less than smaller firms, then growth in the number of large firms may result in increased opportunities for women to enter a wider variety of jobs.

Among nonindustrial firms the association of good performance on the Index with suburban occupations and high degrees of product diversification also strikes an optimistic note, because these appear to be factors which will become increasingly prevalent over time.

These comments do not mean that occupational equality will come easily and quickly. If women are to be hired in larger proportions into higher status jobs, some type of outside enforcement procedure will be required to overcome existing prejudices of society at large, employers, employees, and customers.

The tendency to crowd women into a limited number of occupations makes it clear that simply requiring firms to hire a certain number of women as some proportion of the total work force is not an adequate remedy for occupational discrimination. The tendency for center industrials, and perhaps nonindustrials, to hire only small proportions of women also makes it clear that occupational discrimination will not be eliminated automatically when there are a few women in each occupation. These firms do not appear willing to hire large numbers of women in high-status-high-pay jobs. Basically, the type of outside intervention we are suggsting already exists in the affirmative action concept as set forth in Revised Executive Order #4. This order applies to all federal contractors with contracts valued at $50,000 or more. (See Chapter 5 for a discussion of this order.)

Interest groups which are less than sympathetic to women's rights have expressed some concern that enforcing equal-employment opportunity by examining proportions of women (or minorities) in occupational categories will result in the establishment of a quota system. At this point affirmative action has been applied for such a short time that it is not clear whether it will be a useful aid in solving the problem of occupational discrimination. What does seem clear is that some type of occupational guidelines must be enforced.

This chapter has discussed occupational discrimination within firms in a fairly general way. We have not discussed any occupation or group of occupations in great detail. The following chapter takes an intensive look at occupational discrimination in a prestigious and influential occupation where women comprise a very small share of the work force.[1][2]

4 Women in the Managerial Elite

Women in the managerial elite are few and far between, especially in periphery firms. Among all firms in which we interviewed, approximately 6 percent of all jobs classified as management positions were held by women in 1970. The empirical analysis in Chapter 3 sheds no light on the interfirm comparison of the status of women in management because all occupational categories were combined in the Occupational Index.

In order to gain some insight into the ways women have moved into the managerial elite and the barriers which limit the numbers of women in these top positions, we conducted field research in twelve center and periphery firms. This chapter presents our findings, based on interviews with seventy men and women managers, and integrates them with findings of other studies of management personnel in large and small firms. It presents a profile of characteristics of male and female managers and looks at variations in management style among female executives.

Women in Several Levels of Management

One complicated aspect of any study of managers is that firms include a wide variety of jobs in the broad occupational category of manager. Line formen who direct production workers are included along with senior executives and middle-management personnel.

In a study of sex discrimination in management, the most important question is how women fare in the several levels of management. In Chapter 2 we discussed the fact that center firms are decentralizing their management process. Periphery firms, on the other hand, tend to have a highly personalized style of management. In both large and small firms, however, management jobs may be stratified both vertically and horizontally. When layered vertically within a firm's organizational hierarchy, management personnel fall into line, staff, and senior levels. Important differences also exist among managers when compared horizontally, that is between firms, despite their apparent equality when compared vertically. First-level or line managers within one firm often have substantially different numbers of persons to supervise, along with vastly different spheres of influence on policy. Similar differences abound among middle-management personnel.

In our study, firm officials familiar with management personnel were to select a sample of males and females matched and paired with respect to three broad criteria: level of management responsibility, length of service with the firm, and salary. To the greatest degree possible, our sample controls for both vertical and horizontal strata of each firm's management spectrum. Not surprisingly, we found that it was impossible for these firms to match men and women with respect to all three of these criteria. As Table 4-1 shows, women managers earn significantly lower salaries than men, even though they have longer average length of service with the firm and comparable levels of responsibility in the eyes of senior firm officials.

The twelve firms participating in our field research defined the level of management responsibility in terms of the numbers of persons supervised. The 70 managers in our sample were responsible for 20 to 120 subordinates. Eighty-five percent of these 70 men and women had worked their way up the corporate job ladder in order to acquire these supervisory responsibilities. Their educational backgrounds varied immensely, from high-school diploma to master's degree. The average education for both men and women in this group was one or two years of college.

Other studies of management personnel have reported similar findings about the education of managers. Education is not a good predictor of a manager's vertical placement in a firm's organizational hierarchy.[1] As long ago as the 1950s, this was true. Frank Pierson's study of 562 managers in sixty-seven firms reported a nearly equal share of college graduates in all three levels of management: 61 percent of top management, 63 percent of middle management, and 62 percent of lower management.[2] Even earlier, between 1928 and 1952, middle and top management in industry had comparable educational attainment.[3] In today's big business management circles, educational attainment helps determine a person's promotability, but only along with age and demonstrated performance as a supervisor.[4] The particular major or specialty an aspiring young manager had in college, however, has little to do with their promotability. Liberal arts, business administration, law, life or earth sciences,

Table 4-1
Characteristics of Managers in Matched, Paired Sample

Median	(n-70) Males	Females
Salary	12,000-15,000	9,000-12,000
Age (years)	40-50	40-50
Years of Schooling Completed	Some College	Some College
Marital Status	Married with dependents	Single with no dependents
Number of Years with the Company	6-9	9-12

Source: Field interviews during spring and summer, 1972, in twelve firms.

technical sciences, and engineering enhance one's perceived promotability about equally.[5] Despite the wide variety in educational backgrounds of persons now holding management jobs, the most frequent reason given for the rareness of women in management is the rareness of qualified females, in terms of education and experience.

Once an aspiring manager is inside a firm, his or her speciality matters little in tipping the scales in his favor when management promotions are made. But when firms recruit, graduate business school preparation is attractive to leading firms. However, only within the last decade have the most prestigeous business schools encouraged women students. In 1971 the Harvard Business School boasted 29 women graduating with a class of 754. Seven women completed graduate work at the University of Chicago Business School that year in a class of 280. Several Stanford Business School graduates were among the women managers in junior executive training programs in banks and manufacturing concerns participating in our study. Edward Robie's survey of placement officers at female under-graduate colleges revealed some reluctance on the part of female students to prepare for business careers. Despite the oversupply of teachers, women undergraduates still prepare for these careers.[6] Some resocializing of girls through educational institutions is essential if women are to develop enough interest in management to sell themselves to those firms whose doors are open.

At the highest level of management, where significant decision-making occurs, speciality in both education and experience seems to be more important. In most center firms, a large share of key management jobs in corporate head-quarters are held by professionals who direct others as well as practice their particular speciality. Lawyers, actuaries, and systems analysts have firm foot-holds in the management hierarchy. Cynthia Epstein argues, in our view rightly, that these fields are prime ones for developing female access to higher management.[7]

Some verification of our evidence that center firms give women a larger share of management jobs comes from two recent studies. One survey in 1970 of 163 firms found that large firms use more women in first- and middle-level management jobs than small firms. Top management jobs present a different story. Table 4-2 shows that 27 percent of large firms use over a tenth of their female employees in first-level supervisory jobs, compared to only 20 percent of small firms. Moreover, 11 percent of large firms use over a tenth of their female work force in middle-management positions, compared to only 8 percent of small firms. Table 4-3 presents these findings of the Bureau of National Affairs survey of ninety-eight large and sixty-five small firms. Only 1 percent of large firms use more than a tenth of their women in top management, compared to 6 percent of small companies as shown in Table 4-4.

A second source of support for our findings is the research of Eleanor Schwartz.[8] Her survey of six hundred firms included both large and small firms and sampled nine hundred business executives, one third of whom were women.

Table 4-2

Percentage of Women in First-level Supervisory Jobs

	All Companies	Small Companies	Large Companies
0	20%	26%	16%
Less than 1%	13%	17%	10%
1-2%	19%	17%	20%
2-5%	8%	6%	9%
5-10%	7%	7%	7%
Over 10%	23%	20%	27%
No Response	8%	6%	10%

Source: The Bureau of National Affairs, Inc., "Women and Minorities in Management and in Personnel Management," *Personnel Policies Forum*, Washington, D.C.: The Bureau of National Affairs, Inc., Survey No. 96, December 1971. Reprinted by special permission from Bulletin to Management, copyright 1971 by The Bureau of National Affairs, Inc., Washington, D.C.

Table 4-3

Percentage of Women in Middle Management

	All Companies	Small Companies	Large Companies
0	44%	63%	34%
Less than 1%	14%	11%	17%
1 to 2%	12%	9%	13%
2 to 5%	6%	3%	6%
5 to 10%	6%	1%	8%
Over 10%	9%	8%	11%
No Response	9%	5%	12%

Source: The Bureau of National Affairs, Inc., "Women and Minorities in Management and in Personnel Management," *Personnel Policies Forum*, Washington, D.C.: The Bureau of National Affairs, Inc., Survey No. 96, December 1971. Reprinted by special permission from Bulletin to Management, copyright 1971 by The Bureau of National Affairs, Inc., Washington, D.C.

Table 4-5 from the Schwartz survey shows that a larger number of big than small businesses employ women in 6 percent or more of all management jobs.

The distribution of women in management according to level of responsibility, as we noted earlier, is more important than their share of all jobs a firm labels "management" positions. Table 4-6 presents a comparison of large and small firms with respect to this distribution, based on the traditional vertical stratification of management jobs. Neither group of firms in this survey used over 2 percent of the female work force in senior management. Seventy big businesses used between 6 and 25 percent of female employees in middle-

Table 4-4
Percentage of Women in Top Management

	All Companies	Small Companies	Large Companies
0	76%	85%	70%
Less than 1%	4%	1%	6%
1-2%	5%	5%	5%
2-5%	1%	0%	2%
5-10%	1%	0%	1%
Over 10%	3%	6%	1%
No Response	9%	3%	13%

Source: The Bureau of National Affairs, Inc., "Women and Minorities in Management and in Personnel Management," *Personnel Policies Forum*, Washington, D.C.: The Bureau of National Affairs, Inc., Survey No. 96, December 1971. Reprinted by special permission from Bulletin to Management, copyright 1971 by The Bureau of National Affairs, Inc., Washington, D.C.

Table 4-5
Extent to Which Women Are Employed at Management Level Among Respondees

Percent of Management Personnel Who Are Women	Respondee Classification					
	Big Businesses		Small Businesses		Women in Management	
	N	%	N	%	N	%
0-2	25	31	28	43.7	50	33.3
3-5	20	24	14	21.9	32	22.4
6-10	15	19	11	16.9	20	13.9
11-15	10	12	6	8.7	15	11.0
16-25	7	9	3	6.3	9	6.3
26-40	3	4	1	2.5	10	7.5
41-Over	1	1	0	0	8	5.6

Source: Survey conducted among selected sample of big businesses, small businesses, and women in management.
Source: Eleanor Brantly Schwartz, *The Sex Barrier in Business*, Atlanta: Publishing Services Division, School of Business Administration, Georgia State University, 1971, p. 64. Reprinted by permission from Publishing Services Division, School of Business Administration, Georgia State University.

management positions. Only forty-three small businesses had equivalent levels of utilization. Fifty large firms used 16 percent or more of their women workers in first level management, compared to only twenty-four small firms.

Our interviews with corporate level officers in twelve firms leads us to believe

Table 4-6

Distribution of Women in Management According to Level of Responsibility

	Respondee Classification											
Management Level % Range	Big Businesses						Small Businesses					
	Senior		Middle		First Level		Senior		Middle		First Level	
	N	%	N	%	N	%	N	%	N	%	N	%
0-2	81	100	0	0	0	0	63	100	0	0	0	0
3-5	0	0	11	13.6	0	0	0	0	20	31.7	0	0
6-10	0	0	30	37.0	1,1	13.6	0	0	23	36.5	0	0
11-15	0	0	30	37.0	20	24.7	0	0	10	15.9	14	22.2
16-25	0	0	10	12.4	40	49.3	0	0	10	15.9	25	39.7
25-Over	0	0	0	0	10	12.4	0	0	0		9	14.3

Source: Survey conducted among selected sample of big businesses and small businesses.

*For example, 30 (or 37 percent) of the big business firms reported that 6-10 percent of their women in managerial positions were at the middle level of management.

Source: Eleanor Brantly Schwartz, *The Sex Barrier in Business*, Atlanta: Publishing Services Division, School of Business Administration, Georgia State University, 1971, p. 65. Reprinted by perimission of Publishing Services Division, School of Business Administration, Georgia State University.

that one of the reasons large firms use women in management more fully than small firms is their ability to disperse female managers. Large firms are better able than small firms to place women managers in units where most subordinates are women. Moreover, women are likely to be less threatening to men with whom they compete for management positions in such units.

Both large- and small-firm officials explain obstacles to using more women in management in terms of their lack of education and experience—and their greater proclivity for turnover. This latter argument appeals especially to male managers who remember losing young women workers to marriage or to relocation because of spouses. Yet almost no firms keep turnover statistics by sex. All firms complain of losing bright young men to other jobs in other locations but do not use that as a reason for not hiring men.

The following sections compare the characteristics of male and female managers and describe the four styles of management which we identified in the course of our interviews.

Characteristics and Perceptions of Male and Female Managers

In both center and periphery firms, women managers have longer service with the firm and less average salary than men with comparable levels of responsibility. The women tend to be older than the men. All surveys of management personnel done within the past ten years report that women tend to be single with no dependents while men tend to be married with dependents. The most interesting differences between the men and the women are somewhat more subtle.

More men and women managers in small firms perceive themselves to be treated equally than do men and women managers in large firms. This fact emerged from our field research as well as from a widely cited study by Bowman, Worthy, and Greyser.[9] How can patterns of perception diverge from what seem to be facts? Large firms utilize women more fully in management jobs, certainly at lower and middle levels. But managers themselves believe men and women to be equally treated in more small firms than in large firms. Our interviews suggested that visibility and dispersion are again the best explanations. The few women in management are much more visible in a small firm, and much less dispersed among all management personnel. This perceptual puzzle may arise because the more personalized work setting affords women in small firms greater visibility.

No perceptual split with factual reality exists, however, on the question of special advantages for women. As Table 4-7 shows, data from the Bowman, Worthy, and Greyser study show both male and female respondents perceiving "moderate but not equal" opportunity for women, regardless of firm size. Our interviews of seventy managers revealed that the women are more optimistic about their own chances of getting into the executive suite than men. Forty percent of the male managers argued that a woman has virtually no chance of getting to the top of the managerial elite. Only a fourth of the women managers took such a pessimistic view.

Perceptual patterns of men and women managers are remarkably similar with respect to sex stereotyping. One of the barriers women in management must surmount is the preference by both men and women to work for males. This preference arises from sex stereotypes and emotional responses which are culturally derived. Polls by Louis Harris suggest that women's attitudes about themselves provide a strong influence maintaining the present structure of the job market. Working women prefer a male boss to a female boss 8 to 1.[10] We found no significant difference among male and female managers with respect to their reliance on selected stereotypes about the sexes. Insufficient variance between male and female responses to questions found in Table 4-8 prompted us to pool the two sets of data.

Having found similar patterns of sex-stereotypical thinking among male and female managers, Rosalind Loring and Theodora Wells observe:

Stereotypes may be viewed . . . as screens that block out other experiences or information which would lead to personalized responses. Stereotypic screens filter responses to women and provide certain consistent patterns of thinking and reacting.[11]

It was not the women's mothers who taught them to tuck tail, to feel less, to be second. It was in the air they breathed. The new generation of women in

Table 4-7

Variations in Opportunities for Women in Management

| | As Seen By Men | | | | | As Seen By Women | | | | |
	Distinct Advantage	Equal	Moderate (But Not Equal)	Very Little	Virtually None	Distinct Advantage	Equal	Moderate (But Not Equal)	Very Little	Virtually None
Size of Company										
Large	0	12	43	34	9	0	8	40	33	11
Medium	0	8	46	39	3	1	15	57	20	1
Small	1	21	36	26	12	3	36	35	13	5
Job Level										
Top management	0	2	12	45	40	0	4	21	45	25
Middle management	0	7	41	45	7	0	15	53	23	4
Lower management	1	29	56	12	1	3	42	42	5	1
Nonmanagement	6	60	30	2	0	20	49	20	2	2

Source: Garda W. Bowman, N. Beatrice Worthy, and Stephen Greyser, "Are Women Executives People?" *Harvard Business Review*, Vol. 43, No. 4, July-August 1965, p. 25. ©1965, by the President and Fellows of Harvard College; all rights reserved.

Table 4-8

Management Perception of Sex-specific Worker Traits: Percentage Distribution of Responses to Selected Questions (n = %)

Perception of Trait	Yes %	No %	Don't Know %	(%)
Finds generalized sex-linked work traits	55.7	35.4	8.9	100
Finds women less decisive than men	38	57	5	100
Finds women less aggressive than men	39	54.7	6.3	100
Finds women less committed to a career than men	66.6	24.4	9.0	100
Finds women less likely to use independent judgment than men	36.7	50.6	12.6	100
Finds women less interested in seeking responsibility than men	41	46.2	12.8	100
Finds women less skilled as negotiators than men	25.3	63.3	11.4	100
Finds women less competitive than men	48.7	36.3	15	100
Finds women less productive on the job than men	17.6	29.7	52.7	100
Thinks women have higher turnover rates than men	57.7	33.3	9.0	100
Thinks women have higher absentee rates than men	56.3	33.7	10	100
Finds workers resent or dislike having female supervisors because they are female	36.8	9.2	54	100

Source: Interviews of matched paired sample of male and female managers in twelve firms, during spring and summer, 1972.

management may be in better psychological shape about being women, and may have a better environment in which to be women.

The psychoanalytic literature is full of explanations of why women would accept the same stereotypes about themselves that men accept. Sex differences in achievement motivation for American youths are significant. Women fear success, but only in situations emphasizing "masculine" characteristics—leadership, abrasive competition, and self-assertiveness. Management jobs are seldom done well by persons lacking leadership and self-assertion. In laboratory studies, gifted women achieve their potential in noncompetitive, independent working situations.[12]

For their part men have their own fears about women managers.

Perhaps a bad conscience on the part of male-dominated society may explain the anxious fantasy that if women gain increased power they might impose a matriarchy as virulent as the extant patriarchy. Men may fear also the highly mythologized "feminine" emotionality and unpredictability, which may account for women being regarded as nuisances.[13]

However, if our interviews are representative, psychoanalytic interpretations of this kind are overdrawn. Nearly all male managers conveyed genuine respect for the women whose administrative talents they had come to admire. While women managers who are good lady bosses are seen as exceptions to the rule, they enjoy considerable esteem from their male colleagues in both center and periphery firms. A large majority of respondents to Schwartz's survey from both large and small businesses had found women in management to be decisive, capable of firing subordinates when necessary, and unwilling to use feminine wiles to achieve business objectives. Half the officials from both large and small firms felt that the major obstacle women in management faced was in hiring good employees. Schwartz's data on this point confirm the theory that discrimination against women in management runs from employee to employer, rather than the reverse.[14] Ray Killian found women who had refused promotion to management jobs because they anticipated this very difficulty.[15]

Our analysis of characteristics of male and female managers revealed another difference between the two groups. Nearly all male managers in our sample reported that they handled men and women subordinates differently. All of the women managers believed that they dealt with men and women in the same way. A branch manager of a large commercial bank, having held many supervisory positions in the bank, described his handling of subordinates in these terms:

I have learned over the years to present criticism to my girls somewhat differently from the way I present it to my men. A man will respond to a dressing down by addressing his work directly. A woman needs a more subtle approach. I arrange the interview so that I discuss the criticism of her work in the middle of our conversation with plenty of time afterwards to discuss other things. I have learned that this approach helps prevent her from pouting for two or three days and losing that work time.

The majority of men in management had encountered relatively few women subordinates whose motivation was sufficiently high to carry a demanding supervisory job. When women take their own careers more seriously, men will respond in kind, they argued.

Our sample of women managers had taken their careers seriously indeed, and evidenced pride in their accomplishments. Although their philosophies of management varied more than the males', they all believed that they supervise men and women essentially the same. About two thirds of the women managers supervised predominantly female staffs. Many of these women believed that resentment from the women whom they superseded in the course of their own advancement into management was far greater than resentment from men. A highly paid systems analyst, supervising over sixty data-processing specialists, found the men more receptive to her role than the women. One middle aged woman who had moved from a secretarial job to chief of a mortgage loan division in a large insurance firm described her experiences:

The men supported me one hundred percent. My old girl friends still in the [secretarial] pool didn't speak to me for months after my promotion was announced. I simply had to take all that in stride. Some of the old gang still don't want to be friends.

A number of women managers offered explanations for this pattern. A female boss will be equally businesslike with men and women subordinates. Women who have related in an "office-wife" manner to their bosses miss that relationship with a woman boss. Their response is resentment. Methods of dealing with this response and with the production requirements of management jobs varied more among the women. Our sample of men in management emulated the prevailing supervisory style in their particular firm. The sample of women contained many mavericks whose success had hinged on going somewhat against the company grain as a manager. They tended to be different from the firm's male management image. This difference was their claim to fame in the firm.

Variations in Management Styles
Among Female Executives

Our sample of women managers fell into four groups with respect to style. About a third used a productive, somewhat overcontrolling approach to administration. Another third were receptive bosses, following a permissive philosophy of handling subordinates. About a sixth of the women adopted a detached, almost undercontrolling style in their relations with their staffs. The last sixth of our sample displayed exploitative attitudes toward their positions, paying little attention to the administrative tasks at hand in an attempt to use their job as a stepping stone to a better one. Much more homogeneous, the male sample fell easily into only two of these classifications. About three fourths of the men adopted an exploitative style, delegating to a deputy the nuts and bolts of administration. The remaining men best fit the productive, overcontrolling management type.

This typology of management styles grew out of our interviews both with the managers themselves and with their subordinates. So often work associates have quite different images of their bosses than their bosses have of themselves. Our study revealed very little of this disparity, probably because all managers had held their present positions for over five years. Their reputations within the firm were established. Not surprisingly, both the men and women displayed most of the traits generally associated with success in management: desire for achievement; drive for mobility; acceptance of authority figures; decisiveness; assertiveness; practicality—a tendency to look at facts; and a strong fear of failure.

Regardless of style, the women had relied on mentors more than the men. Both in making the break into management and in establishing their credibility as managers, the women had been dependent on sponsors. Most had ridden on the coattails of young male executives. Well over half of the women had been recommended initially for their present jobs by men who had moved up or out of the same job.[16]

The productive management style takes the form of a highly task-oriented attitude toward the job. These managers evaluate themselves and their subordinates in functional terms. The approach of a forty-six-year-old systems analyst with two sons in college is a good example of this style. Chief of the data processing division of a large chemical firm, she supervises over a hundred men and women programmers, card punchers, and hardware and software specialists.

Her understanding of the unit's function is to deliver the various computer runs on time. Repeat, *on time.* She knows little about her employees other than their output at work and has no interest in getting involved on a friendly basis with them. She keeps very accurate records of their use of time. Her subordinates find her overcontrolling, but comfortably predictable. They never ask for any favors or special privileges. They would not get them if they asked. There are many rules to live by in her shop. But if you live by them and produce for her, she will deal fairly with you. She sees no special need for greater equality of opportunity for women in her unit. She is quick to point out, and quite correctly, that computer science has been one field in which women have done very well. She is a prime example of this. So she doesn't plan to make any special concessions to the women. They will continue to be handled exactly as the men are handled.

A second group of women managers have become successes by using a receptive, somewhat permissive style. These women have reputations as good old girls in their firms. They are well liked, if not known for their efficiency. They see to it that the job gets done, but put a high premium on keeping their subordinates happy. One of the results is a tendency to delegate poorly—they avoid conflict in the office by pitching in and doing the work of subordinates if pressures are mounting to meet a deadline. Many men in management expressed dismay at this particular "female" style of running an office. From their point of view, this style is an overaccommodating one, indulged in by women who are too anxious to please everybody. The employees of lady bosses who use this style tell quite a different story. Unanimous praise for these women as managers comes from their subordinates. A number of such subordinates had turned down promotions and transfers in order to make less money in an office where they are happy. They expressed a firm belief that their boss cared about them personally as well as professionally. The special loyalty these women executives are able to secure from their people must be the envy of other executives.

The manager of a large cafeteria in a retail store used this receptive approach especially well. Like others with this style, she believes strongly that the use of fear as a motivating device is inherently counterproductive. Reliance on positive incentives and reinforcement for good performance has enabled this twenty-six-year-old woman to supervise thirty-three men and women far older than she. She is intimately familiar with the family lives of all her subordinates and she works just as hard as they do. They all expressed the feeling that she respects their wisdom and maturity. She is receptive to their suggestions about changing procedures or work assignments. She is a youthful master of the light touch.

Only about a sixth of the women managers in our sample used the detached style. The detached manager delegates so well that the place is running itself—or so it seems. She maintains an aloof relation to the staff she supervises without controlling directly. Her form of administrative control is indirect and subtle. She gives the appearance to her staff of being above the fray and inaccessible to them. This appearance is not deceiving with respect to her inaccessibility. She sees her staff by appointment only and insulates herself carefully from them on a day-to-day basis. Her evaluation of them seems to include, among other things, their ability to solve their own work problems.

An aeronautical engineer in a large aircraft firm is prototypical of this style. Quite happy with her position in the management hierarchy, she enjoys the autonomy which this detachment affords her. The men who report to her do so by being autonomous themselves. She thinks that they are content to have her negotiate the major federal contracts for the firm, because she is an old hand at it. Her manner is extremely low key, though not austere. She communicates with her staff primarily in writing. Her closest subordinate reported that engineers entering the unit often were given a list of her publications. If they initially doubted her competence, their doubts disappeared when they spent an afternoon in the firm library.

A fifty-seven-year-old physician in the medical unit of a film plant also uses this style in supervising nurses, lab technicians, and junior physicians. Like the other women in this group, she seems to have great confidence in herself at work. All the proving has been done. She is invulnerable to her subordinates' problems about accepting a woman boss. Her staff doesn't know whether they like her or not, but they accept her role. She is available only for the special cases and they know it.

More common among men than women, the exploitative style characterized a sixth of our sample of women. These women viewed their present jobs as launching pads to the next level in the management hierarchy. Hence, they are very concerned about looking good to their own superiors in the firm. They seek visibility for their unit and tend to capture the credit for successes themselves. The blame for failures is systematically delegated to subordinates, who not infrequently feel scapegoated. These managers do not consider it in their interest to assist junior people in the development of their own potential. There is nothing in it for them. They want employees who will make them look good and do as they are told. They are very threatened by subordinates who are highly ambitious in their own right. Their staffs tend, as a result, to be of mediocre caliber. The manager often plays one subordinate against another in a conscious attempt to discharge any hostilities that could be directed at herself. She is not particularly concerned about employee morale. If they are unhappy, why don't they leave?

A thirty-two-year-old woman supervising forty-eight men and women in the credit department of a large clothing manufacturer makes no bones about using this approach. She has her career pattern clearly drawn and has no intention of being stuck in this particular division the rest of her life. Men in management refer to her as the barracuda type. Her employees admit to fear of her. She is extremely adept at neutralizing ambitious subordinates who gain visibility which she wants for herself. It is her practice to send them on extended field assignments as a neutralizing tactic. She is authoritarian and officious in manner to her subordinates. To her superiors in the firm, she is solicitous and self-effacing. Her competence is widely acknowledged, as is her personality.

These four styles suggest that successful women in the managerial elite are an interesting lot. Their diversity offers hope to women interested in management careers. Certainly both center and periphery firms have enough flexibility to accommodate a number of individual styles in management positions. The center firm is especially able to do so, because women in management can be sprinkled throughout the firm. However, this dispersion of female management personnel neutralizes any collective action on their part.

In the course of our study we found no evidence that firms have any reason to move larger numbers of women into positions of real power and influence within the firms. However, if the average size of firms continues to grow, perhaps more women can move into management positions in these very large firms where women managers can be dispersed throughout the many company facilities. But even if the growth of large firms leads to some improvements in women's access to management jobs, the pace may be extremely slow. We indicated in the conclusion to Chapter 3 that one way of accelerating the movement towards occupational equality, and especially the movement of women into high-level managerial positions, is through government intervention. The next chapter deals with the steps already undertaken by the federal government to bring about equal opportunity in employment. An analysis of federal outlays for equal employment purposes follows a discussion of federal statutes and executive orders relating to sex discrimination.

The Role of the Federal Government in Equal Employment Opportunity

Federal Statutes, Executive Orders, and Equal Employment Opportunity

During the 1960s there was a growing awareness in the United States of the economic potential of women and of the existence of barriers which placed limits on women's participation in the economy. Studies like the one conducted by the President's Commission on the Status of Women focused attention on the fact that a number of forces, including court decisions, statutes, the prevailing attitudes on women's capabilities and work patterns, and practices of employers, employment agencies, and unions, had contributed to the discriminatory treatment of women workers.[1] In fact, until recently discriminatory practices against women have been so widespread and pervasive that they were often regarded as normal.

This chapter is primarily a discussion of the federal statutes and executive orders which have been enacted and issued since 1960 in an effort to end the discriminatory treatment of women workers. Prior to 1960 there were two types of legislation which affected women's employment status. At the federal level, the Fair Labor Standards Act of 1938 established a floor for wages paid to persons engaged in interstate commerce and to persons involved with the production of certain types of goods. While the minimum wage was a useful step to assist women in gaining a more equitable share of the rewards of their labor, it was not designed to deal with such issues as equal employment opportunities and equal pay for equal work. The second type of legislation that affected women was a series of state laws which regulated the number of hours women could work, the weight of objects they could lift, and the types of occupations in which they could be employed. While the original purpose of these state laws may have been the protection of women from extremely long hours of work and from physically demanding and hazardous occupations, such statutes kept women from earning overtime pay which they needed and from filling positions for which they were qualified.

Some proponents of equal rights for women have believed that their goal could be achieved through judicial interpretation of the equal protection clause of the United States Constitution. In 1963 the President's Commission on the Status of Women supported this view that the principle of equality could become established through the use of the 5th and 14th amendments.[2]

However, the courts have failed to interpret the equal protection and due

93

process guarantees of the 5th and 14th amendments as prohibiting discrimination against women. In 1908 the Supreme Court, combining arguments based on the physical capabilities of women and historical patterns of male dominance, concluded, "[woman] is properly placed in a class by herself" as a subject for legislation.[3] This paternalistic attitude of placing women in a protected class was reflected in a Supreme Court decision in 1961. A Florida law held that men could be excluded from jury service only if they applied for such an exclusion. Yet women could participate in jury service only if they filed *for* such a right. In this case, *Hoyt v. Florida*, the Supreme Court upheld the state law and found sex-related characteristics a reasonable basis for excluding women from exercising the full rights of citizenship.[4] Another recent case illustrating the treatment of women as a separate class was the case of *Williams v. McNair.* All of the state universities of South Carolina are coeducational except two, and maintenance of these two schools by sex was challenged. The District Court found that there was reasonable justification for this separation by sex and the Supreme Court, without a finding, affirmed the lower court decision.[5]

The cases cited illustrate that to date the equal protection concept has not been an effective tool for attacking sex-distinguishing statutes. A second and more fruitful approach to employment equality for women has been the enactment of new federal statutes and the issuance of executive orders related to hiring, pay, and advancement. The two major pieces of legislation were the Equal Pay Act and the Civil Rights Act of 1964; the two Executive Orders were Order 11375 and Revised Order 4.

Equal Pay Act of 1963

The Federal Equal Pay Act was signed in 1963 as an amendment to the Fair Labor Standards Act of 1938. The movement to establish the principle of equal pay for equal work began in the United States in 1868, when the National Labor Union Convention demanded equal pay for federal and state government employees. The first comprehensive Equal Pay Bill was introduced to the Congress in 1945 and similar measures were submitted in each Congress until the bill was passed on June 10, 1963.

The passage of the bill as an amendment to the Fair Labor Standards Act meant that white-collar employees were not protected because they were exempt from coverage of the Fair Labor Statute. However, in June of 1972 equal-pay provisions were extended to cover about fifteen million executive, administrative, and professional employees and outside salespeople.

The equal-pay provision prohibits employers from discriminating on the basis of sex in payment of wages for jobs requiring equal skill, effort, and responsibility and performed under similar working conditions. Another provision of the Act prohibits labor organizations from causing or attempting to cause an employer to discriminate against an employee. The Act does not prohibit wage differentials based on a bona fide seniority system, a merit system, or a system in which earnings are based on quantity or quality of production.

One of the best-known equal-pay cases is *Hodgson v. Wheaton Glass Company*, in which the court ordered a payment of more than $900,000 to women inspector-packers who had been paid less than men for substantially equal work. This case established the principle that work need only be substantially equal in order to compare the wages of men and women employees.[6]

The Wage and Hour and Public Contracts Division of the Department of Labor administers and enforces the equal-pay law. The definition of "wages" used by this agency is remuneration for employment, which includes most fringe benefits. Attempts are made to settle cases out of court and such settlements have been possible in about 95 percent of the cases to date. The enforcement procedures under the Equal Pay Act seem to be fairly effective because the Wage and Hour Division employs about one thousand compliance officers and the Division is authorized to make investigations of establishments, whether a specific complaint is received or not. These routine compliance investigations are made in about one in twenty establishments each year, amounting to approximately 75,000 establishments in 1972. Between 1963 and 1972 about $46 million has been found owing to over 110,000 employees, nearly all of whom were women. Roughly 85 percent of this money was owed to women whose wages were close to the minimum wage.

Civil Rights Act of 1964

With the passage of the Civil Rights Act of 1964 it became unlawful for employers, unions, and employment agencies to discriminate on the basis of sex, race, color, religion, or national origin. This law currently applies to businesses and unions with fifteen or more workers, employment agencies, state and local governments, and educational institutions, with the exception of religious institutions. More than 75 percent of the labor force, not including self-employed persons, is covered by the Act.

One important exception contained within the Act is the bona fide occupational qualification. This qualification permits discrimination based on sex if it is reasonably necessary to the operation of a particular business or enterprise. While this exception is vague and somewhat unclear, the courts and the agency charged with the enforcement of the employment section of the Civil Rights Act have held that the bona fide occupation qualification as to sex should be narrowly interpreted. For example, refusal to hire because of assumptions about the comparative employment characteristics of women in general or stereotyped characterizations of women or preferences of coworkers, employers, clients, or customers is not a justifiable application of the bona fide occupation qualification exception.

In *Weeks v. Southern Bell Telephone and Telegraph Company* the burden for justifying a bona fide occupational qualification was placed emphatically on the employer. This case involved a woman excluded from a job as a switchman because of a state weight-lifting law. The case went before an appeals court on the question of the meaning of "bona fide occupational qualification."[7] The appellate decision was that there was no justification for sex as a bona fide occupational qualification on the grounds that physical activity or late night hours were coincident with job performance. "Title VII rejects just this type of romantic paternalism as unduly Victorian and instead vests individual women with the power to decide whether or not to take on unromantic tasks."[8] The Fifth Circuit Court of Appeals held that "the employer must show a factual basis, as opposed to a commonly held stereotype, for a reasonable belief that all or substantially all members of one sex would be unable to perform the duties of the job safely and efficiently."[9]

Two other cases, *Rosenfeld v. Southern Pacific Co.*[10] and *Bowe v. Colgate-Palmolive Co.*,[11] also narrowly interpreted the bona fide occupational qualification, thus restricting the range of allowable exceptions under Title VII of the 1964 Civil Rights Act.

One case which is somewhat disappointing with respect to its ruling on bona fide occupational qualification is *Phillips v. Martin Marietta Corporation.*[12] The Supreme Court adopted the position that being a woman with preschool-age children would be a valid bona fide occupational qualification if it could be shown that such women have a poorer work record, rather than holding that each case must be treated individually.

The major responsibility for the enforcement of Title VII of the Civil Rights Act (the section related to employment) was given to the Equal Employment Opportunity Commission (EEOC). Until 1972 the EEOC's powers were limited primarily to investigating complaints of employment discrimination and attempting to resolve these practices through discussion and persuasion. In cases where no settlement was reached, the Commission had no independent enforcement power; the aggrieved employee had to take action in the United States district court on his or her own. In cases where there was a pattern of intentional violations by an employer, the U.S. Attorney General was authorized to bring a civil action in the courts. Despite the fact that the Commission did not have enforcement power if conciliation attempts failed, the EEOC investigations and opinions were important in making decisions about intervening in private suits and referring a matter for suit by the Attorney General.[a] Further, good faith

---

[a]It should be noted that the Department of Justice has filed very few lawsuits on behalf of EEOC. In fiscal year 1970 two suits were filed and in fiscal year 1971 only one EEOC case was accepted by the Department of Justice. A partial explanation for the small number of cases accepted by the Department of Justice is that most of the cases which EEOC has submitted for consideration have been at least two years old and at the time of receipt by the Department of Justice the cases have lost their timeliness and relevance.

reliance upon and conformity with EEOC opinions was an absolute defense in any action based on an alleged unlawful employment practice.

In 1972 the enforcement powers of the EEOC were expanded to permit the General Counsel of EEOC, after full investigation, to bring civil suit in a federal court against any employer found to be practicing discrimination on the basis of sex. This new legislation also authorizes the courts to order employers to halt discriminatory practices (cease and desist power) and to remedy past action. The addition of these new powers gives the EEOC more tools with which to fight sex discrimination.

One problem with which the EEOC has been dealing since its establishment is the conflict between state laws regulating the employment of women and the Title VII provisions for equal employment. The initial guidelines on equal employment for women, issued by EEOC in 1965, divided state laws regulating women's employment into two categories: laws providing benefits for women, such as rest periods, and laws which exclude women from employment in certain strenuous or hazardous occupations. Those laws which appeared to fall in the first category were to be considered as a basis for the bona fide occupational qualification exception, but those laws which had ceased to be relevant as protective measures (the second category of state laws) were superceded by Title VII of the Civil Rights Act. The problem with this guideline was that the EEOC was not clear about which laws fell into each of the two categories. In 1969 the EEOC issued a new set of guidelines finding that state legislation had ceased to be relevant to present-day technology or the expanding role of women in the work force and did not take into account the preferences and abilities of individual women.

Court decisions on the conflict between Title VII and state protective laws have been mixed in their conclusions, but the majority of opinions have held that Title VII supercedes state laws which are overly protective and that an employer may not set arbitrary standards with respect to employment of women workers and then invoke the bona fide occupational qualification as an excuse. *Rosenfeld v. Southern Pacific Co.* involved the exclusion of a woman from employment because of a state law restricting the hours a woman could work and the maximum weight a woman could be required to carry. The Court determined that a conflict between Title VII and a state law did exist and ruled in favor of Title VII.[13] Another interesting case relevant to the issue of the conflict between state and federal laws was *U.S. v. Libby-Owens-Ford Co., Inc.* The consent order in this suit decided in favor of federal over state laws and also stated that policies must be instituted both to eliminate present discrimination and to insure that hiring policies are designed to avert future discrimination.[14] Since 1969 a number of state attorneys general held, with the approval of EEOC, that state laws governing hours of work for women were superceded by Title VII of the Civil Rights Act and would not be enforced. Such opinions have been issued by the attorneys general of South Dakota, Pennsylvania, Oklahoma, Michigan, Massachusetts, Missouri, Wisconsin, and Washington and the Corporation Counsel of the District of Columbia.

The current EEOC Guidelines on Discrimination Because of Sex were issued on April 5, 1972. On the issue of the bona fide occupational qualification the guidelines state that the refusal to hire a woman because of sex-based assumptions on the employment characteristics of women in general or because of stereotyped characterizations of the sexes will be considered violations of Title VII. The current guidelines preclude separate lines of progression, separate seniority systems, and classification of a job as "male" or "female." In the area of fringe benefits, such as medical, hospital, accident, life insurance, and retirement and pension plans, it is unlawful to discriminate between men and women with regard to such benefits or to make available benefits for the wives and families of male employees which are not made available for husbands and families of female employees.[15] The guidelines further state that employers may not refuse to hire applicants for employment or terminate employees simply because they are pregnant.[16] Further, any requirement that all pregnant employees cease work at the conclusion of a specified period of months of pregnancy violates Title VII.[17] If a woman is physically unable to work because of pregnancy, miscarriage, abortion, childbirth, and recovery therefrom, she is entitled to the benefits her employer provides for employees generally who are physically unable to work. Such benefits may include sick leave and pay, temporary disability leave and pay, medical and hospital insurance coverage, retention and accrual of seniority, job reinstatement, etc.

EEOC efforts at eliminating employment discrimination have encountered several problems which have severely limited the agency's effectiveness.[18] According to a report by the U.S. Civil Rights Commission, it takes between sixteen months and two years for an individual's charge to move through the EEOC machinery to an attempted conciliation. At the very least this delay renders many cases moot, and, it may make many individuals reluctant to initiate complaints. The backlog of uninvestigated complaints exists not because of administrative inefficiency, but because of the low level of the agency's budget relative to the volume of complaints received.

Second, in those cases where the Commission finds that discrimination has occurred but cannot effect a conciliation, the private complainant has to file suit. Less than 10 percent of these unconciliated cases get into court because the charging parties cannot afford the expense and time of private litigation. The newly founded Women's Legal Defense Fund may help to alleviate this problem.

Third, when the EEOC does effect a conciliation agreement, the inadequate budget afforded the agency has made close monitoring of the implementation of such agreements very difficult. This means that in many cases in which EEOC obtains a conciliation, there is no subsequent review to verify that the agreement is actually put into action.

One recent case involving EEOC illustrates a novel procedure for pursuing equal employment opportunity for women. In 1970 when American Telephone and Telegraph requested a rate increase, EEOC asked the Federal Communications Commission to deny the request on the grounds that the company pursued discriminatory hiring and promotion practices. EEOC linked the increase to discrimination by stating that discrimination resulted in higher turnover rates which caused heavy training costs. In January 1973 EEOC and the Office of Federal Contract Compliance agreed to a lump-sum payment of $15 million to persons who had been objects of discrimination and immediate raises for about 36,000 workers.

Executive Order 11375

This executive Order, which became effective in 1968, prohibits discrimination on the basis of sex in employment by federal contractors and subcontractors and in employment on federally assisted construction. (Approximately one third of the nation's labor force is employed in companies which hold government contracts.) Order 11375 replaced Executive Order 11246, signed in 1965, which had prohibited employment discrimination on several grounds but did not include sex as one of the categories.[b] The guidelines based on Order 11375 prohibit separate seniority rosters for men and women, discrimination based on a woman's marital or child-bearing status, and separate columns of "help-wanted" ads for men and women in newspapers. In addition to the prohibition on discrimination, Order 11375 requires the contractors to take affirmative action to ensure that applicants are employed and that employees are treated during employment without regard to race, color, religion, sex, or national origin. The affirmative action concept was included in Order 11375 because the laws and regulations which simply prohibit discrimination have had little effect on the makeup of the work force. However, there was a problem with the affirmative action section of the order because the content and form of an affirmative action program were not clearly explained.

In order to remedy the confusion over the affirmative action procedure, Order #4 was issued in February 1970. This order specified the steps involved in the establishment of such a program, but women were not included as one of the categories of workers to be included in this review of the work force. Order #4 was revised in December 1971 to include women as one of the groups to be considered in establishing any affirmative action plan.

Currently Revised Order #4 requires that an affirmative action plan include the following elements:

1. An analysis of deficiencies in the contractor's compliance posture, including an examination of job classifications to determine where minorities and women are underrepresented;

---

[b]There have been requirements of equal employment opportunity with regard to race imposed on government contractors since 1941, but as late as 1970 the Civil Rights Commission stated that this type of employment discrimination in the private sector was still prevalent.

2. a plan for corrective action, including numerical goals and timetables where these are relevant;

3. mechanisms for disseminating the policy and measuring the program's effectiveness.

Revised Order #4 applies to all federal contractors and subcontractors who have fifty or more employees and whose federal contract is valued at $50,000 or more. However, companies are not required to submit these affirmative action plans to any federal agencies; the plans are kept in the company's files and are reviewed only in cases of complaints by employees or during the course of periodic compliance investigations. In cases in which the value of the contract is more than $1,000,000, bidders on federal contracts are subject to a review of their affirmative action program prior to the awarding of the contract.

The Office of Federal Contract Compliance in the U.S. Department of Labor is the policy-making agency which issues guidelines in this area. The responsibility for monitoring and compliance investigations is shared by OFCC and seventeen cooperating federal agencies.

There are two mechanisms through which cases of discrimination come to the attention of these agencies; complaints from employees and routine periodic compliance reviews by the federal monitoring agencies. In fiscal year 1971 over 22,000 compliance reviews were made and the target number for 1972 was 44,000. Since only a portion of the contractors are reviewed in any one year, it seems likely that many contractors are not reviewed at all during the life of a contract.

The Department of Defense is the most important of the compliance monitoring agencies, with responsibility for about 30,000 establishments and 75 percent of federal contracts. The size of the Defense Department's compliance staff is indicative of the government-wide situation of inadequate staffing, which inhibits effective civil rights enforcement. In 1970 the Department of Defense had less than 150 compliance officers available to conduct compliance reviews. While an additional 170 compliance positions were added in 1971, the total number was still far too small to permit the annual review of 50 percent of contractors as required by the Office of Federal Contract Compliance.

In cases in which the compliance agencies are not able to rectify discriminatory practices through conciliation and discussion, a show-cause notice can be issued giving the contractor thirty days to comply before proceedings begin which will terminate the contract. During fiscal year 1972 more than six hundred show-cause notices were issued by the agencies monitoring contract compliance efforts. In addition, the OFCC or the cooperating federal agencies can also debar contractors from future contracts and publicly identify non-complying contractors. Executive Order 11375 does not include any sanction less drastic than termination of contracts, and only three contract terminations have ever taken place. The failure to use the sanctions provided in the Executive

Order has lessened the credibility of the government's compliance program and weakened the contract compliance effort.

One complaint that has been expressed by federal compliance officials working with affirmative action plans is that in many cases the final decision on the acceptability of a firm's plan is taken away from the federal equal employment opportunity officials and is made by someone higher up in the federal bureaucracy who agrees to comply with OFCC regulations. Clearly, such actions lessen the credibility of federal civil rights efforts and may make future cases even more difficult to resolve.

In addition to the two federal statutes and two Executive Orders that have been discussed, there have been other developments within the federal government related to women's employment rights. One of the problems encountered in civil rights enforcement has been the lack of a method for determining which firms are most in need of federal investigation of their employment practices; that is, which firms have the poorest level of performance in the area of equal employment opportunity and are most in need of remedial action. In order to help solve this problem of target selection, the Office of Federal Contract Compliance has adopted a model developed by Robert B. McKersie.[19] It should be noted that many of the variables included in the model are quite complicated, which may to some extent limit the ease of its application.

Since 1973 there has been a special section of the publication *Special Analyses of the U.S. Budget* devoted to governmental civil rights activities. In addition, the 1973 Economic Report of the President includes an entire chapter to the economic role of women.[20] While it is gratifying that women's role, and civil rights more generally, are receiving some attention in government documents, words are not a substitute for action.

In another event related to the government's role in matters related to equal employment opportunities for women, in 1972 President Nixon declared that numerical goals must not be applied so as to result in the imposition of quotas. This statement came in response to a letter from the president of the American Jewish Committee expressing concern over the spread of quota systems in education and employment. At present it is not clear what the long-run future of affirmative action plans will be. Is it possible to have goals and timetables that don't involve preferential hiring (that is, some sort of quota), or will various goals exist based on hiring of at least some minimum numbers of minorities and women?

Finally, in 1972 the Equal Rights Amendment for women was passed by the U.S. Congress, forty-nine years after it was first introduced. The ratification of this constitutional amendment would provide a sense of national commitment to the goal of equal rights for women. The amendment embodies a moral judgment that women as a group may no longer be relegated to an inferior position in our society, and implies that equal status can be achieved only by merging the rights of men and women.

In the area of employment this constitutional amendment will provide a mechanism for constitutional challenges to discriminatory employment practices. Until the ERA is ratified and cases have been adjudicated, the overall effect of the amendment on employment opportunities will not be known.

Federal Expenditures for Equal Employment Opportunity

To date the efforts to achieve equal employment opportunities for women have fallen short of the expectations of some of the supporters of this aspect of the civil rights movement. One of the reasons for the rather slow pace of the change is the inadequate outlays to the government agencies charged with the responsibility for implementing the equal employment legislation. The limited budgets for the equal employment agencies have resulted in insufficient staffs to monitor and enforce the legislative directives in the private sector. In order to substantiate this charge of insufficient budgets and staffs, the following section details some of the financial aspects of the federal government's equal employment efforts. It is not possible to separate funds used for enforcement of women's rights from those funds used for enforcement of minority rights, but it is possible to isolate the expenditures in the field of equal employment and to list the expenditures of those agencies most directly connected with the implementation of the major women's employment legislation.

Federal government expenditures for civil rights enforcement were approximately $100 million in fiscal year 1969, $190 million in 1971, and are estimated to be about $521 million in the 1974 fiscal year.[21] Civil rights enforcement activities include protection of such rights as voting, public accommodations, fair housing, and equal employment opportunity in the public and private sectors.

In the 1972, 1973, and 1974 budgets, civil rights expenditures were less than .5 percent of federal outlays for selected social programs. (Selected social programs included outlays for education, manpower, health, income security, housing, civil rights, and reduction of crime.)[22] This low level of financial commitment to civil rights enforcement suggests that civil rights is a low priority item, even among existing social programs.

Expenditures for federal service and private sector equal employment opportunities enforcement amounted to $62 million in 1971, $102 million in 1972, and were estimated to be about $181 million in 1974.[23] Federal service enforcement includes those programs designed to expand employment opportunities for minorities and women within the federal government. Private sector employment includes federal government activities to expand employment opportunities in the private sector.

Among those agencies most directly concerned with expansion of employ-

Table 5-1

Federal Civil Rights Enforcement Outlays by Program Category (in Millions of Dollars)

	1971 Actual	1972 Actual	1973 Estimate	1974 Estimate
Civil rights enforcement:				
Federal service equal employment opportunities	27.80	55.50	70.13	99.59
Military services equal opportunities	5.95	26.16	34.94	51.95
Private sector equal employment opportunities	34.43	46.67	64.35	81.80
Equal educational opportunity	70.30	96.43	74.34	206.42
Fair housing	7.55	11.83	13.80	15.79
Enforcement and investigation	34.15	43.71	49.40	53.64
Program direction, research and information dissemination	4.96	6.17	7.88	8.56
Indian programs	0.40	0.75	0.80	1.10
Civil rights conciliation and prevention of disputes	4.20	5.51	6.60	2.62
Total	189.74	292.73	322.24	521.47

Source: Office of Management and Budget, *Special Analyses of the United States Government: Fiscal Year 1973*, p. 210 and *Special Analyses: Budget of the United States Government: Fiscal Year 1974*, p. 180.

ment opportunities for women, the Equal Employment Opportunity Commission budget grew from about $16 million in 1971 to an estimated $43 million in 1974.[24] In 1974 the federal agencies responsible for federal contract compliance, under Executive Order 11375, will spend about $34 million, which is about double the $16.4 million outlay of 1971.[25] The Department of Labor will spend approximately $2 million in administering the Equal Pay Act in 1974. However, this figure is not an accurate reflection of the resources available for enforcement of the Equal Pay Act because the investigators who enforce this statute are payed from Wage and Hour Division funds.[26]

The low level of commitment to civil rights enforcement, as reflected in federal outlays, can be changed only through the political process.[27] Women's lobby groups have recently integrated their work with other civil rights interest groups, such as the Civil Rights Leadership Conference. This coalition approach could avoid further splintering of civil rights interests and enable an even more broadly based lobby effort to materialize. White House commitment is critical if more aggressive pattern settlements are to become typical. Since women have great potential political influence sheerly numerically, the creation of concensus among women is the task for the coming decade. Civil rights officials in federal agencies have long noted that women are the most disunited group covered by these laws and regulations. While this observation may be an overstatement, it is likely that women can secure more favorable resource allocation for programs designed to aid them than they now get. The following chapter discusses policy in somewhat more detail and suggests some new avenues for research in this field.

Summary and Recommendations

Summary

This chapter summarizes the findings of our work and offers some ideas for further research on occupational discrimination. It also includes our conclusions about the additions and changes to federal policy that will make equal employment opportunities a reality.

There has been a marked expansion in the female labor force in the past quarter century. In April 1972, nearly 33 million women in America worked for pay outside their homes. They represented 43.4 percent of the female population 16 years of age and older.

A major part of the explanation of this increase in number and proportion of working women appears to be the attempt to maintain the purchasing power of U.S. households. The increase of the proportion of working women does not appear to have been preceded or accompanied by changes in attitudes towards working women.

The entrance of more women into the world of work has not resulted in any significant restructuring of the sex composition of occupations. Women continue to be concentrated in jobs classified as women's work. In addition to the sex-typing of occupations, which has resulted in fairly definite conceptions of what is "proper" women's work, women are concentrated in certain occupations because they are believed to have a low level of commitment to work. Employers are unwilling to risk placing women in high-status or responsible positions because they may leave or be unwilling to invest sufficient time in their jobs. Women have been especially excluded from professional, managerial, and blue-collar positions.

The beliefs and conditions just described provide an explanation for occupational discrimination throughout the economy. But the degree of occupational discrimination varies throughout the economy. Some firms discriminate more than others. The goal of the statistical tests included in this book is to explain the differences in occupational discrimination among firms.

We tested a number of different hypotheses which we believe would be systematically related to interfirm differences in the extent of occupational discrimination against women. We tested whether variations among firms in the number of their jobs which were perceived as "women's work" explains the proportion of women they hire and the jobs into which the women are placed. Second, was there any aspect of a firm's relationship with the federal government or with the public which was related to the extent of its occupational discrimination? The third hypothesis we tested was whether the structural dimensions of a firm, such as size, strength, and power, were systematically related to its extent of occupational discrimination. In particular, we wanted to know if the theory of business-dualism provided useful insights into the extent of interfirm differences in occupational discrimination. We were also interested in discovering if there were any systematic relationships between innovativeness of management practices, location of corporate headquarters, extent of urbanization of production facilities, or degree of administrative autonomy of the employing unit and differences in extent of occupational discrimination among firms. Among the industrial firms in our sample we found that the degree of occupational discrimination is related to the proportion of jobs that are female sex-typed and the centrality of firms. Firms engaged in light manufacturing and food processing have large numbers of female sex-typed jobs and the large numbers of women within these firms are concentrated in these occupations. The largest industrial firms employ women more widely throughout their occupational structures, perhaps because these firms have so many locations and subdivisions, and a small proportion of women can hold responsible high-status positions without threatening either their superiors or coworkers. The one public policy indicator which was related to occupational discrimination was Extent of Participation in Social Programs. Firms which have considerable occupational equality between men and women also participate in a large number of social programs.

Among nonindustrial firms, good performance on the Occupational Index for those with moderate proportions of women is related to suburban and small-town location of facilities, high degree of product diversification, little incidence of civil rights and labor relations litigation, and government contracts with nondefense agencies. For nonindustrials with large, or small, proportions of female employees, the occupational distribution of women is related to the proportion of white-collar jobs in the firms and to management innovation. Unlike industrials, in nonindustrial firms, we did not find evidence to support the hypothesis that the dualistic nature of firms is systematically related to the extent of occupational discrimination. There is some support for the occupational-crowding hypothesis, although the evidence was not nearly as strong as in the industrial sample.

Our study of discrimination in one of the highest-status occupation within these firms—management—indicated that women hold more lower-level and middle-management positions in large firms than in small firms. There is limited evidence that women hold more top management positions in small firms, perhaps because many of these firms are family-owned firms in which the women managers are also a part of the owner-families.

Women managers in our study possessed a wider variety of management styles than did men. Only about one sixth of the women managers displayed exploitative attitudes toward their positions in an attempt to use their jobs as stepping stones to better ones. Three fourths of the men adopted this style. The difference may be the result of the more limited expectations of most women managers to achieve more responsible positions.

One problem that women managers faced was employee acceptance. Neither men nor women were particularly happy about being supervised by women. Women's entry into management will remain difficult so long as employees are resistant to women managers.

Our examination of equal employment law and practice indicated that current federal efforts in this field are hampered by shortages of staff who could pursue complaints and undertake investigations.

Research Issues

A number of important issues related to occupational discrimination require additional research.

One important research question is whether some theory of the structure of the U.S. economy, other than business dualism, provides more useful insights into the characteristics of firms that are associated with occupational discrimination. The theory of business dualism, which stratified firms into two groups on the basis of asset level, sales level, and level of employment, provided useful insights into occupational discrimination among industrial firms but was not helpful in explaining interfirm differences in extent of occupational discrimination in nonindustrial firms. Perhaps another structural theory which included different indicators would be especially helpful in explaining variations in discrimination among nonindustrial firms.

All of the firms in our sample had more than one thousand employees. Additional research on occupational discrimination in small firms seems warranted. The characteristics associated with occupational discrimination might be considerably different for small firms than for large ones.

Another interesting expansion of this work would be an examination of occupational discrimination in banks and insurance companies, which were two types of firms not included in our sample.

One of our indicators measured the extent of international sales of a firm, and in the industrial sample the firms with sizeable overseas sales volume performed well on the Occupational Index. However, considerably more work needs to be done on the impact on women of the growth of multinational corporations. There are important questions relating to the ability of the U.S. government to regulate domestic multinationals and the facilities within the U.S. belonging to foreign firms. The future of the occupational structure of the United States, and the impact of multinationals on that structure, also must be studied with respect to its effect on women's employment opportunities.

There is an even broader question associated with the future of the U.S. economy. As the United States moves into a postindustrial era, how will the changes in the occupational structure, the nature of work, and the length of the work week affect women workers? As the economy shifts from a manufacturing to a service base, will women's occupational opportunities be better or worse than they are now?

Public Policy

Our work gave us some understanding of the role of public policy in providing equal employment opportunities for men and women. These insights provided a basis for a broad range of policy recommendations.

In terms of macroeconomic policy, a vigorous pursuit of the goal of full employment would provide women with increased opportunities to enter those occupations in which they are currently underrepresented. When traditional sources of labor dry up, employers may be more willing to use women to fill positions that they usually fill with men. If there are very few male managers looking for jobs, an employer might be more willing to hire a woman for a management position.

Full employment also benefits the women who are part-time workers, who might be most vulnerable to being fired during a recession.

The existence of occupational crowding indicates that occupational discrimination must be attacked on a disaggregated, within-firm basis. Simply looking at the female proportion of a firm's labor force is not adequate equal employment enforcement, because firms might continue to crowd females into a limited number of occupations. We support federal equal employment efforts which focus on the proportion of women in each occupational category. In this context, it is imperative that equal employment enforcement efforts are provided with adequate budget and staff to accomplish the tasks of investigation and conciliation.

One approach to equal employment enforcement that might be effective for those firms which apply to government agencies for rate increases is tying the rate increases to an affirmative action employment plan (we have called this pattern regulation). This type of approach was introduced in the AT&T case which was settled in January 1973. When AT&T applied to the Federal Communications Commission for authority to increase their rates, the Equal Employment Opportunity Commission and the Office of Federal Contract Compliance asked that the increase be denied because discriminatory practices of the company had been a factor leading to higher operating costs. Perhaps this approach could be expanded so that rate increase requests presented to state regulatory agencies would also be tied, where appropriate, to changes in employment practices.

The ratification of the Equal Rights Amendment will be an important milestone in the women's rights movement. Its adoption will indicate a commitment to equal rights and will provide a constitutional basis for challenges to discriminatory practices. The constitutional basis is especially important because the Supreme Court has shied away from affirming that sex is the same suspect classification as race in discrimination cases.

Labor organizations have expressed opposition to the Equal Rights Amendment on the grounds that its passage may be used as an excuse to abolish minimum-wage laws and that nothing in the amendment prohibits the reduction of benefits. The responses of the supporters of ERA have been that the existing state laws do not really offer substantial protection and benefits for women, and women's employment status would be greatly improved if they received the benefits and opportunities now available to men.

Continued improvement of women's employment opportunities require support from the highest levels of government. Women can help to assure this support by increasing their participation in the political process. The President and Members of Congress will be responsive to pressure for equal employment opportunities exerted through the party system and special-interest groups.

Women should also continue to exert pressure for legal precedents by appealing increased numbers of cases to the Supreme Court.[1] While the cost of litigation is a tremendous burden for an individual, the combined financial resources of large numbers of women might result in some path-breaking legal decisions.

We support some new initiative to promote more women into managerial positions. Our study indicated that women who become managers are forced to rely heavily on the support of mentors to assist them in breaking into the managerial ranks. Firms should be encouraged, perhaps with government assistance, to develop training programs and personnel development policies which would identify and assist those women who, but for mentors, would already have become managers.

The most important changes which will bring about equal employment opportunities lie beyond the realm of federal enforcement. They are changes in social attitudes about women and work. We need to rethink our ideas about what is "proper" women's work and the commitment of women to their jobs. We must reevaluate the way in which we educate young women and the occupations we encourage them to enter. Women managers must be more accepted by their peers and by those they supervise. We should also revise our beliefs that women's questions are less important than those of minorities, and that women's rights are in some cases competitive with those of other disadvantaged groups. To the extent that women are successful in their efforts to be viewed as individuals, each with unique capabilities, all workers should profit from this struggle.

Notes

Notes

Chapter 1
An Overview of Woman's Role
in the American Economy

1. Charlotte P. Gilman, *Women and Economics*, New York: Harper and Row, 1966.

2. Janet M. Hooks, *Women's Occupations Through Seven Decades*, Washington, D.C.: Government Printing Office, 1948, pp. 206-7.

3. *The Status of Women in the American Economy: Report to the United States Senate*, Washington, D.C.: Government Printing Office, 1910.

4. A number of studies document these trends. See for example Howard V. Hayghe, "Work Experience of the Population in 1969," *Monthly Labor Review*, Vol. 91, No. 2, February 1968; Vera C. Perrella, "Women and the Labor Force," *Monthly Labor Review*, Vol. 91, No. 2, February 1968; Jacob Schiffman, "Marital and Family Characteristics of Workers, March 1960," *Monthly Labor Review*, Vol. 84, No. 4, April 1961; Elizabeth Waldman, "Marital and Family Characteristics of the Labor Force," *Monthly Labor Review*, Vol. 93, No. 5, May 1970; U.S. Department of Labor, Women's Bureau, *Why Women Work*, Washington, D.C.: Government Printing Office, 1970.

5. U.S. Department of Labor, Bureau of Labor Statistics, *Employment and Earnings*, Washington, D.C.: Government Printing Office, May 1972.

6. Leland J. Axelson, "The Marital Adjustment and Marital Role Definitions of Husbands of Working and Nonworking Wives," *Marriage and Family Living*, 25, May 1963; James N. Morgan et al., *Productive Americans*, Ann Arbor: University of Michigan, 1966.

7. See Valerie Oppenheimer, *The Female Labor Force in the United States*, Berkeley: The University of California Press, 1970.

8. *1969 Handbook on Women Workers*, Women's Bureau Bulletin 294, Washington, D.C.: Government Printing Office, 1969, p. 95.

9. Ibid.

10. Valerie K. Oppenheimer, "The Female Labor Force in the United States: Factors Governing Its Growth and Changing Composition," Ph.D. dissertation, University of California, Berkeley, 1966.

11. Valerie K. Oppenheimer, "The Sex-Labeling of Jobs," *Industrial Relations*, VII, May 1968, p. 225.

12. Oppenheimer, "The Female Labor Force in the United States."

13. David Gordon, *Theories of Poverty and Underemployment*, Lexington, Mass.: Lexington Books, 1972, p. 48.

14. Prepublication tabulations from the 1970 U.S. Census of Population.

15. Ibid.

16. Gary S. Becker, *The Economics of Discrimination*, Chicago: University of Chicago, 1957.

17. Eli Ginzberg, *The Negro Potential*, New York: Columbia University Press, 1956; and Elton Rayack, "Discrimination and the Occupational Progress of Negroes," *Review of Economics and Statistics*, Vol. 43, May 1961.

18. Finis Welch, "Black-White Differences in Returns to Schooling," paper presented at a Conference on Discrimination in Labor Markets, Princeton University, October 7-8, 1971.

19. Joan Robinson, *The Economics of Imperfect Competition*, London: Macmillan and Company Ltd., 1934, pp. 301-14.

20. Martin Bronfenbrenner, "The Economics of Collective Bargaining," *Quarterly Journal of Economics*, 53, August 1939, pp. 535-61.

21. F.Y. Edgeworth, "Equal Pay to Men and Women for Equal Work," *Economic Journal*, 32, December 1922, pp. 431-57.

22. Barbara Bergmann, "The Effect on White Incomes of Discrimination in Employment," *Journal of Political Economy*, Vol. 79, March/April, 1971, pp. 294-313.

23. Lester Thurow, *Poverty and Discrimination*, Washington, D.C.: Brookings Institution, 1969, pp. 66-93.

24. *1969 Handbook on Women Workers*, pp. 76-80.

25. Jan Pen, *Income Distribution; Facts, Theories, Policies*, New York: Praeger, 1971, pp. 266-67.

26. Kenneth Arrow, *Some Models of Racial Discrimination in the Labor Market*, RM-6253-RC, Santa Monica, California: The Rand Corporation, February 1971, p. 22.

27. Robert F. Averitt, *The Dual Economy; The Dynamics of American Industry Structure*, New York: W.W. Norton and Company, 1968. Copyright 1968 by Robert T. Averitt.

28. Ibid., pp. 66-70.

29. Peter Doeringer and Michael Piore, *Internal Labor Markets and Manpower Analysis*, Lexington, Mass.: D.C. Heath, 1971.

30. Michael Piore, "The Dual Labor Market: Theory and Implications," in D.M. Gordon, ed., *Problems in Political Economy: An Urban Perspective*, Lexington, Mass.: D.C. Heath, 1971.

31. Sar A. Levitan, Garth Mangum, and Ray Marshall, *Human Resources and Labor Markets*, New York: Harper and Row, 1972, p. 219.

Chapter 2
Selection of Variables and Firms

1. *Sixth Annual Report: Equal Employment Opportunity Commission*, Washington, D.C.: Government Printing Office, 1972, p. 5.

2. See Joseph E. Stiglitz, "Approaches to the Economics of Discrimination," *American Economic Review: Papers and Proceedings*, Vol. LXIII, May, 1973, pp. 287-95.

3. Employment data are from 1970 E.E.O.-1 forms made available by the U.S. Equal Employment Opportunity Commission. Income data are from *Income in 1970 of Families and Persons in the U.S. Current Population Survey*, Table 60, P-60, No. 80, Washington, D.C.: U.S. Bureau of the Census, U.S. Department of Commerce, 1971, p. 129.

4. See Barbara R. Bergmann and Jerolyn R. Lyle, "The Occupational Standing of Negroes by Areas and Industries," *Journal of Human Resources*, 5, Fall 1971, pp. 411-33; Jerolyn R. Lyle, *Differences in the Occupational Standing of Black Workers Among Industries and Cities*, Washington, D.C.: Government Printing Office, 1970; Jerolyn R. Lyle, "Factors Affecting the Job Status of Workers with Spanish Surnames," *Monthly Labor Review*, Vol. 96, April 1973, pp. 10-16.

5. The AT&T agreement is now the classic case in point. Other cases of importance in the development of relief system guidelines are those in which the courts have emphasized prospective relief. See *Rosen v. Public Service Electric & Gas Co.*, 409 F. 2d 775 (C.A. 3 1969); *Bowe v. Colgate-Palmolive*, 416 F. 2d 711 (C.A. 7 1969); *Parham v. Southwestern Bell*, 433 F. 2d 421, 60 LC 9297, 2 FEP Cases 40 (E.D. Ark. 1969); *Jenkins v. United Gas Corp.*, supra; *U.S. v. Bethlehem Steel*, supra.

6. Relevant cases are *Quarles v. Philip Morris*, 297 F. Supp. 505 (E.D. Va. 1968) and *Hicks v. Crown Zellerback Corp.*, 1969 LRRM 2005 (1968).

7. The income weights used for computing this index for the firms are for males: Officials and Managers—$11,430; Professionals—$10,722; Technical Workers—$10,722; Sales Workers—$7,992; Office and Clerical Workers—$7,585; Craftsman—$8,580; Operatives—$6,671; Laborers—$5,027; Service Workers—$4,337.

8. "Special Report on Multinational Companies," *Business Week*, December 19, 1970, p. 2.

9. U.S. Tariff Commission, *Report to the President on Economic Factors Affecting the Use of Items 807.00 and 806.30*, Washington, D.C.: Government Printing Office, 1970, p. 163.

10. Averitt, *The Dual Economy: The Dynamics of American Industry Structure*, p. 18.

11. Data are from "The Fortune Directory," *Fortune*, May 1971.

12. Ibid.

13. Ibid.

14. Ibid.

15. Ibid.

16. Ibid.

17. "The Fortune Directory," *Fortune*, July 1966 and May 1971.

18. "The Fortune Directory," *Fortune*, May 1971.

19. *Surveys of Mergers in Manufacturing and Mining*, Washington, D.C.: Federal Trade Commission, 1971. Firms that either acquired or were acquired by manufacturing or mining firms are included. Thus, retailing firms, transportation and utilities companies are to some extent covered.

20. Ibid.

21. Data are from *Standard and Poors*, 1968-70, and annual reports of firms.

22. See Federal Reserve Bulletin for breakdown of the index of industrial production into output categories. This typology is based on a collapse of these categories into only seven. The categories are assigned ascending ordinal values as follows: mining, oil, chemicals, rubber, clay, glass, containers, lumber, primary and fabricated metals; machinery and related products; transportation and utilities; textiles, paper and printing; food and home consumer nondurables; retailing.

23. The specific descriptions of firms relying on these technologies in the mid-1960s are in Averitt, *The Dual Economy*. Other data sources include *Standard and Poors*, 1966-70; company annual reports over the same period; and selected periodical articles.

24. *Standard and Poors*, 1968-70, annual reports of firms, 1965-70. In addition to these primary sources, a number of secondary sources were of great help in scaling. The most useful were those by Raymond Vernon and his colleagues at the Harvard Project on Multinationals. See Raymond Vernon, *Sovereignty at Bay: The Multinational Spread of U.S. Enterprises*, New York: Basic Books, 1971.

25. "The Fortune Directory," *Fortune*, May 1971.

26. Ibid.

27. 1970 E.E.O.-1 forms.

28. Ibid.

29. Ibid.

30. See Ivar Berg, *Education and Jobs: The Great Training Robbery*, New York: Columbia University Press, 1971.

31. Data are from periodicals indexed in *Funk and Scott Index of Business and Corporations*, 1965-70. Case summaries from Commerce Clearing House and the Bureau of National Affairs series were also used.

32. Ibid.

33. Ibid.

34. The Office of Federal Contract Compliance, U.S. Department of Labor provided these data.

35. Ibid.

36. A number of firms sent us information on their activities in these areas. The U.S. Department of Labor provided information on activities of a large group of firms. For the remaining firms we surveyed articles indexed from a wide variety of business periodicals in *Funk and Scott Index of Business and Corporations*, 1965-70.

37. Data sources include a wide variety of periodicals indexed in *Funk and Scott Index of Business and Corporations*, 1965-70.

38. *Standard and Poors* and Annual Reports of firms.

39. Ibid.

40. E.E.O.-1 data were crosschecked with company annual reports and with *Standard and Poors* to verify the nature of the employing unit.

41. Dean Morse, *The Peripheral Worker*, New York: Columbia University Press, 1969, p. 79.

42. Averitt, *The Dual Economy; The Dynamics of American Industry Structure,* op. cit., p. 123.

43. *Business Week*, No. 1909, April 2, 1966, p. 91.

44. New York City Commission on Human Rights, *Women's Role in Contemporary Society*, New York: Avon, 1972, p. 221.

Chapter 3
Occupational Discrimination in Industrial
and Nonindustrial Firms

1. Irma Adelman and Cynthia Taft Morris, "Analysis of Variance Techniques for the Study of Economic Development," *The Journal of Development Studies*, VIII, October 1971, p. 98.

2. Thurstone, *Multiple Factor Analysis*, p. 61.

3. See H.F. Kaiser, "The Varimax Criterion for Analytic Rotation in Factor Analysis," *Psychometrika*, September 1958.

4. George W. Mayeske, Carl E. Wisler, Albert E. Beaton, Jr., Frederic D. Weinfeld, Wallace M. Cohen, Tetsuo Okada, John M. Proshek, and Kenneth A. Tabler, *A Study of Our Nation's Schools*, Washington, D.C.: U.S. Department of Health, Education and Welfare, Office of Education, 1971.

5. Irma Adelman and Cynthia Taft Morris, "Who Benefits from Economic Development," unpublished paper, p. 7.

6. J. Sonquist and J. Morgan, *The Detection of Interaction Effects*, Ann Arbor, Michigan: Institute for Social Research, University of Michigan, 1964, pp. 5-6.

7. Valerie K. Oppenheimer, "The Sex-Labeling of Jobs," *Industrial Relations*, VII, May 1968. For further discussion of the sex-typing of occupations see an article by Francine Blau Weisskoff, "Women's Place in the Labor Market," *American Economic Review, Papers and Proceedings*, LXII, May 1972, pp. 161-66.

8. Juanita Kreps, *Sex in the Marketplace: American Women at Work*, Baltimore: Johns Hopkins Press, 1971, pp. 35-36.

9. Harriet Zellner, "Discrimination Against Women, Occupational Segregation and the Relative Wage," *American Economic Review, Papers and Proceedings*, LXII, May 1972, pp. 157-60.

10. Raymond S. Franklin, "A Framework for the Analysis of Interurban Negro-White Economic Differentials," *Industrial and Labor Relations Review*, Vol. 21, April 1968, pp. 367-74.

11. Barbara Bergmann, in an article on racial discrimination, links occupational crowding of blacks with employer discrimination. See Barbara Bergmann, "The Effect on White Incomes of Discrimination in Employment." *Journal of Political Economy*, Vol. 79, March/April 1971, pp. 294-313.

12. Several of our colleagues read earlier drafts of this chapter and provided helpful suggestions on methodology. To Gary Fromm, Nancy Barrett, Howard Wachtel, Ronald Mueller, and George Mayeske we are grateful. Several students at the American University provided valuable research assistance in data preparation and analysis. We thank Jean A. Pierre Courbois, John Berg, Richard Crutchfield, Charlotte Myers, and Martina Lewis for their help. We also thank Bennett Harrison of the Massachusetts Institute of Technology for his encouragement to us in applying the technique of factor analysis to the problem of discrimination.

Chapter 4
Women in the Managerial Elite

1. A now classic general work of direct relevance to this point is Ivar Berg, *Education and Jobs: The Great Training Robbery*, New York: Praeger, 1971.

2. Frank C. Pierson, *The Education of American Businessmen*, New York: McGraw-Hill Book Company, Inc., 1968, p. 102.

3. W. Lloyd Warner and James C. Abegglen, *Occupational Mobility in American Business and Industry*, 1928-52, Minneapolis: University of Minnesota Press, 1955.

4. Fred Luthans, James W. Walker, and Richard Hodgetts, "Evidence on the Validity of Management Education," *Academy of Management Journal*, Vol. 12, December 1969, pp. 451-57.

5. Ibid., pp. 456-57.

6. Edward A. Robie, "Challenge to Management," in *Corporate Lib: Women's Challenge to Management*, Baltimore: The Johns Hopkins Press, 1973, pp. 9-29.

7. Cynthia F. Epstein, *Woman's Place: Options and Limits in Professional Careers*, Berkeley: University of California Press, 1970.

8. Eleanor Brantly Schwartz, *The Sex Barrier in Business*, Atlanta: Bureau of Business and Economic Research, School of Business Administration, University of Georgia, 1971.

9. Garda W. Bowman, N. Beatrice Worthy, and Stephen Greyser, "Are Women Executives People?" *Harvard Business Review*, Vol. 43, July-August, 1965, pp. 14-28, 166-78.

10. Louis Harris and Associates, *The Virginia Slims American Women's Opinion Poll*, New York, 1971.

11. Rosalind Loring and Theodora Wells, *Breakthrough: Women into Management*, New York: Van Nostrand Reinhold Company, 1972, p. 131. See also George J. McCall and J.L. Simmons, "Social Perception and Appraisal," *Down to Earth Sociology*, James M. Henslin, ed., New York: The Free Press, 1972, pp. 45-49.

12. M. Horner, "Sex Differences in Achievement Motivation," unpublished Ph.D. dissertation, University of Michigan, 1968. M. Horner, "Femininity and Successful Achievement: A Basic Inconsistency," *Feminine Personality and Conflict*, 55, 1970.

13. Barbara K. Cavanagh, "A Little Dearer Than His Horse: Legal Stereotypes and the Feminine Personality," in Harrison William Fox, Jr. (ed.), *Contemporary Issues in Civil Rights and Liberties*, New York: MSS Educational Publishing Company, Inc., 1972, p. 34.

14. Schwartz, *The Sex Barrier in Business*, pp. 80-82.

15. Ray A. Killian, *The Working Woman: A Male Manager's View*, American Management Association, Inc., 1971, pp. 47-55, 179-80.

16. Other writers have reported this greater tendency for women to use mentors. See Margaret Hennig, "What Happens on the Way Up," *The MBA* (Master of Business Administration), March 1971, pp. 8-10. Margaret Cussler, *The Woman Executive*, New York: Harcourt, Brace, and Company, 1958, pp. 17-26. Charles Orth and Frederic Jacobs, "Women in Management; Pattern for Change," Harvard Business Review, Vol. 49, July-August, 1971, pp. 139-47. Douglas W. Bray, "The Assessment Center: Opportunities for Women," *Personnel*, Vol. 48, September-October, 1971, pp. 30-34.

Chapter 5
The Role of the Federal Government
in Equal Employment Opportunity

1. The President's Commission on the Status of Women, *American Women*, New York: Charles Scribner's Sons, 1965, pp. 19-20.

2. Ibid., pp. 212-13.

3. *Muller v. Oregon*, 208 U.S. 412 (1908) at 422.

4. *Hoyt v. Florida*, 368 U.S. 57 (1961).

5. *Williams v. McNair*, 401 U.S. 951 (1971) affig 316 F Supp 134 (D.C. 1970).

6. *Schultz v. Wheaton Glass Company*, 421F. 2nd 259 (Third Cir. 1970), certiorari denied, 398 U.S. 905 (1970).

7. *Weeks v. Southern Bell Telephone and Telegraph Co.*, 408 F 2d 228 (th Cir. 1969).

8. Ibid., at 236.

9. B.A. Brown et al., "Employment Discrimination and Title VII of the Civil Rights Act of 1964," *Harvard Law Review*, Vol. 84, March 1971, p. 1179.

10. *Rosenfeld v. Southern Pacific Co.*, 293 F Supp. 1219 (C.D. Cal. 1968).

11. *Bowe v. Colgate-Palmolive Co.*, 416 F. 2d 711 (7th Cir. 1969).

12. *Phillips v. Martin Marietta Corp.*, 400 U.S. 542 (1971).

13. *Rosenfeld v. Southern Pacific Co.*, 293 F Supp. 1219 (C.D. Cal. 1968).

14. *U.S. v. Libby-Owens-Fort, Co., Inc.,* 3 E.P.O. P 8052 (N.D. Ohio 1970). For EEOC rulings and recent court decisions on state protective laws see the following: Sec. 1604.2, EEOC Rules and Regulations, 37 Fed. Reg. 6835 (Apr. 5, 1972); *Schaeffer v. San Diego Yellow Cab Inc.*, 4 EPD para. 7882 (C.A. 9 1972); *Rosenfeld v. Southern Pacific Co.*, 3 EPD para. 8247 (C.A. 9 1971); *Richards v. Griffith Rubber Mills*, 300 F. Supp. 338 (D.C. Ore. 1969); *Local 246, Utility Workers Union of America v. Southern California Edison Co.*, 3 EPD para. 8100 (C.D. Calif. 1970); *Caterpillar Tractor Co. v. Grabiec*, 63 LC para. 9522 (D.C. Ill., 1970); *Ridinger v. General Motors Corporation*, 3 EPD para. 8175 (S.D. Ohio 1971); *Garneau v. Raytheon Co.*, 3 EPD para. 8153 (D.C. Mass. 1971).

15. In connection with sex discrimination in retirement and pension plans, see *Bartmess v. Drewrys U.S.A., Inc.*, 444 F.2d 1186 (C.A. 7 1971), cert. denied 92 S.Ct. 2746 (U.S.S. Ct. 1971); *Rosen v. Public Service Electric and Gas Co.*, 409 F.2d 775 (C.A. 3 1969), 3 EPD para. 8242 (D.C.N.J. 1971), 3 EPD para. 8073 (D.C.N.J., 1970), 3 EPD para. 8074 (D.C.N.J. 1970). In *Fillinger v. East Ohio Gas Co.*, 4 FEP Cases 73 (D.C. Ohio 1971), involving a mandatory retirement program that forced women to retire three years earlier than men, the court awarded the plaintiff $10,000 in damages, which represented the three years of unpaid wages she would have earned.

These decisions conform to the principles expressed in Sec. 1604.9 of the Commission's Guidelines on Discrimination Because of Sex.

16. For a decision finding it a violation of Title VII to discharge an unwed woman because she became pregnant, see *Doe v. Osteopathic Hospital of Wichita, Inc.*, 334 F. Supp. 1357 (D.C. Kansas 1971).

17. See *Schattman v. Texas Employment Commission*, 4 EPD para. 7679 (C.A. 5 1972), rev'g and remanding 3 EPD para. 8146 (W.D. Tex. 1971).

18. The material in the remainder of this section on the EEOC relies heavily on three reports issued by the U.S. Commission on Civil Rights: *Federal Civil Rights Enforcement Effort: A Report of the United States Commission on Civil Rights, 1970* (Washington, D.C.: Government Printing Office, 1970); *The Federal Civil Rights Enforcement Effort: One Year Later* (Washington, D.C.: Government Printing Office, 1971); *The Federal Civil Rights Enforcement Effort: A Reassessment* (Washington, D.C.: Government Printing Office, 1973).

19. Robert B. McKersie, *Employment Patterns in an Urban Labor Market: The Chicago Experience*, Washington, D.C.: Government Printing Office (for the U.S. Equal Employment Opportunity Commission), 1972.

20. For a discussion of this chapter on women see an article by Barbara R. Bergmann and Irma Adelman, "The 1973 Report of the President's Council of Economic Advisers: The Economic Role of Women," *American Economic Review*, LXIII, September 1973.

21. Office of Management and Budget, *Special Analyses of the United States Government: Fiscal Year 1973*, Washington, D.C.: Government Printing Office, 1972, p. 209; Office of Management and Budget, *Special Analyses: Budget of the United States Government; Fiscal Year 1974*, Washington, D.C.: Government Printing Office, 1973, p. 180.

22. Office of Management and Budget, *Special Analyses of the United States Government; Fiscal Year 1973*, p. 116; Office of Management and Budget, *Special Analyses: Budget of the United States Government; Fiscal Year 1974*, p. 102; and U.S. Bureau of the Budget, *Special Analyses Budget of the United States Government*, Washington, D.C.: Government Printing Office, 1971, p. 116.

23. Office of Management and Budget, *Special Analyses of the United States Government; Fiscal Year 1973*, p. 210; and Office of Management and Budget, *Special Analyses: Budget of the United States Government; Fiscal Year 1974*, p. 180.

24. Office of Management and Budget, *Special Analyses of the United States Government; Fiscal Year 1973*, p. 223; and Office of Management and Budget, *Special Analyses: Budget of the United States Government; Fiscal Year 1974*, p. 195.

25. Office of Management and Budget, *Special Analyses of the United States Government; Fiscal Year 1973*, p. 213; and Office of Management and Budget, *Special Analyses: Budget of the United States Government; Fiscal Year 1974*, p. 185.

26. Office of Management and Budget, *Special Analyses of the United States Government; Fiscal Year 1973*, p. 214.

27. For an excellent recent study of public policy in this field see Irene L. Murphy, *Public Policy on the Status of Women*, Lexington, Mass.: Lexington Books, D.C. Heath and Co., 1973.

Chapter 6
Summary and Recommendations

1. In a Supreme Court decision issued in May 1973 (*Frontiero v. Richardson*), four of the majority justices stated that "classifications based on sex, like classifications based on race, alienage and national origin, are inherently suspect and must therefore be subjected to close judicial scrutiny." Perhaps this case and *Reed v. Reed* are part of a new era in which women will no longer be viewed by the law as a separate class.

Bibliography

Annotated Bibliography of Readings on Women

Woman's Place in Society

Arnott, Catherine, "Married Women and the Pursuit of Profit," *Journal of Marriage and the Family*, vol. 34, no. 1, February 1972, pp. 22-131.

Among educated women, freedom of role choice is replacing the norm of predetermined roles for married women. Today, women seek and remain in roles which maximize their profit.

Barth, Ernest A.T., and Walter B. Watson, "Social Stratification and the Family in Mass Society," *Social Forces*, vol. 48, no. 2, March 1967, pp. 392-402.

The authors examine the implications of differences in occupational status between husband and wife.

Benston, Margaret, "The Political Economy of Women's Liberation," *Monthly Review*, vol. 21, no. 4, September 1969, pp. 13-27.

Women must be regarded as belonging to a class in the Marxian sense. This class is defined by their specific relation to production—their work has use-value but no exchange value since they are responsible for nonmarket household production. It is from this relation to production that their inferior status arises.

Bernard, Jessie, *The Sex Game*. Englewood Cliffs, N.J.: Prentice-Hall, 1968.

Sex roles are affected by changes in the technology of work and family life. As a result, the roles of the sexes and their relations must be reevaluated with each generation. The fact that old values die hard tends to creat conflict within society.

Bernard, Jessie, "The Status of Women in Modern Patterns of Culture," *Annals of the American Academy of Political and Social Science*, vol. 375, no. 1, January 1968, pp. 3-14.

Two obstacles stand in the way of equality between the sexes—woman's obligations as a mother and her refusal to accept a new role. The author examines the impact of equality on our culture.

Bloustein, Edward J., "Man's Work Goes from Sun to Sun, but Woman's Work is Never Done," *Psychology Today*, vol. 1, no. 10, March 1968, pp. 38-41.

The popular belief that a woman can successfully combine family and career is a myth. Given our current social and family structures, such an undertaking is possible only for a few.

Boserup, Esther, *Woman's Role in Economic Development*. New York: St. Martin's, 1970.

Traces the changes in woman's role and status with modernization. The bibliography (pp. 263-75) details the vast literature on women in less developed countries.

Cassara, Beverly Benner, ed., *American Women: The Changing Image*. Boston: Beacon Press, 1962.

All contributors point to the need for men and women to reject the traditional views and stereotypes that distort perception of women's role in society. Stress is placed on the value of woman's work at home and the barriers to equal opportunities for women in the labor market.

Collins, Randall, "A Conflict Theory of Sexual Stratification," *Social Problems*, vol. 19, no. 1, Summer 1971, pp. 3-21.

A system of stratification by sex superimposed over stratification based on power, property, and status results in discrimination against women. Sexual roles are explained in terms of a basic struggle for power and the resources available to man and woman in this conflict depend on the type of social structure.

Coser, Rose Laub, and Gerald Lokoff, "Women in the Occupational World: Social Disruption and Conflict," *Social Problems*, vol. 18, no. 4, Spring 1971, pp. 535-53.

Woman is forced to be the caretaker of the family and to depend for income and prestige on a man. When she works it is important that her success not be publicized to avoid conflict in the familial system. The authors show a more rational system of role and status ascription can be devised which would greatly reduce conflict and increase family cohesion.

Degler, Carl N., "Revolution Without Ideology: The Changing Place of Women in America," *Daedalus*, vol. 93, no. 2, Spring 1964, pp. 653-70.

The absence of an ideology legitimating woman's work outside the home has blunted the effectiveness of women's demands.

Edstein, Gilda F., and Arline L. Bronzaft, "Female Freshmen View Their Roles as Women," *Journal of Marriage and the Family*, vol. 34, November 1972, pp. 671-72.

A plurality of the freshmen respondents saw their role in fifteen years as that of "a married career woman with children." These respondents were primarily from upper-middle class or working class backgrounds.

Erikson, Erik, "Inner and Outer Space: Reflections on Womanhood," *Daedalus*, vol. 93, no. 2, Spring 1964, pp. 582-606.

We have to redefine the identity of the sexes within the context of the nuclear age. The importance of equality may well reside in the need for the values that women have always stood for (realism, responsibility, resourcefulness, devotion) to be represented in the decision-making process.

Farber, Seymour M., and Roger M.L. Wilson, eds. *The Potential of Women*. San Francisco: McGraw-Hill, 1963.

The book is a transcript of discussions held at the University of San Francisco as one of the symposiums on "Man and Civilization."

Gavron, Hannah, *The Captive Wife*. London: Routledge and Kegan Paul, 1966.

The author focuses on the confusion and ambivalence that surround woman's and society's perception of the housewife's role in society. The study is based on interviews of working-class and middle-class wives.

Gilman, Charlotte P., *Women and Economics*. New York: Harper & Row, 1966.

This classic work, originally published in 1898 by Small, Maynard and Company, Boston, analyzes the social constraints which limit the ability of women to achieve their potential in the economy.

Hacker, Helen Mayer, "Women as a Minority Group," *Social Forces*, vol. 30, October 1951, pp. 60-69.

How apt is the designation "minority group" for women? The author suggests that women have a minority group status and proceeds to apply to women some of the sociological concepts used in the study of minority groups (i.e., social distance, race relations cycles, marginality, etc.).

Johnstone, Elizabeth, "Women in Economic Life: Rights and Opportunities," *Annals of the American Academy of Political and Social Science*, vol. 375, no. 1, January 1968, pp. 102-14.

Women's role in the economy is changing as a result of numerous forces. Despite the lessening of discrimination, there are still barriers to the efficient utilization of women's potential. Two essential steps must be taken: improving vocational guidance and training for girls and adapting employment opportunities to the needs of women with family responsibilities.

Jones, Beverly, "Capitalism in Action: The Oppression of Women," in Tom Christoffel, et al., eds., *Up Against the American Myth*. New York: Holt, 1970, pp. 296-310.

Neither men nor women understand the oppression to which women are subjected in a capitalistic system. Even radical women fail to perceive the nature of this oppression, because they are generally single, or if married, have no children, and because society treats the radical women with less discrimination.

Knudsen, Dean D., "The Declining Status of Women: Popular Myths and the Failure of Functionalist Thought," *Social Forces*, vol. 48, no. 2, December 1969, pp. 183-93.

Suggests a gradual decline in the status of women measured in terms of occupation, income, and education. Perpetuation of discrimination results from women's passivity and institutional rigidity, which in turn stem from established preconceptions regarding sex roles.

Odenwald, Robert P., *The Disappearing Sexes*. New York: Random House, 1965.

A clear specification of sex roles is sorely lacking in our society. The women's liberation movement may exacerbate this problem to the extent that the drive for equality has led many to proclaim that there was no difference between the sexes.

Packard, Vance, *The Sexual Wilderness*. New York: McKay, 1968.

There is considerable confusion today about the roles for each sex.

Parkin, Frank, *Class Inequality and Political Order*. New York: Praeger, 1971.

In contrast to conditions in socialistic states, inequalities in market economies are more subtle and complex. Two interlocking processes determine the patterns of distribution: the allocation of rewards to the various positions in society and the ascription of positions among individuals. There are two approaches to equality: either the relationship between position and reward must be severed or individuals must have equal opportunities to achieve alternative positions. Women are not a subordinate class because their status is determined by their family position.

Rowntree, Mickey and John, "More on the Political Economy of Women's Liberation," *Monthly Review*, vol. 21, no. 8, January 1970, pp. 26-32.

Equal access to job outside the home and equal pay can only come about if equality in nonmarket activity is also achieved. There is an inherent contradiction between woman's traditional status within the nuclear family and free wage-labor under capitalism.

Reische, Diana, ed., *Women and Society* (from *The Reference Shelf*, vol. 43, no. 6). New York: The H.W. Wilson Co., 1972.

This is an anthology of contemporary periodical articles dealing with such topic areas as women in the marketplace, social and historical perspectives on women, and biological and social roles.

Spiegel, Jeanne, *Sex Role Concepts: A Selected Annotated Bibliography*. Washington: Business and Professional Women's Foundation, 1969.

The bibliography contains almost one hundred items, including books, articles, and dissertations.

U.S. Department of Labor, Women's Bureau, *Exploding the Myths*. Washington: U.S. GPO, 1967.

This report of a conference held at UCLA contains discussions on popular myths as to sexual differences in abilities, on emerging opportunities for women and on discrimination.

Women's Liberation

Beauvoir, Simone de, *The Second Sex*. New York: Knopf, 1953.

The noted philosopher and author's classic discussion of woman's place in society.

Decter, Midge, *The New Chastity and Other Arguments Against Women's Liberation*. New York: Coward, McCann & Geghegan, Inc., 1972.

The author raises interesting questions about some of the more radical assumptions and goals of the women's liberation movement.

Flexner, Eleanor, *Century of Struggle*. Cambridge: Belknap Press, 1959.

Traces the history of the woman's rights movement in the United States.

Friedan, Betty, *The Feminine Mystique*. New York: Norton, 1963.

Contains analysis of popular magazines and of the role concepts for women transmitted through these media.

Ginzberg, Eli, and Alice M. Yohalem, eds., *Corporate Lib: Women's Challenge to Management*. Baltimore: The Johns Hopkins University Press, 1973.

This anthology presents the major papers that were presented at a conference on women's challenge to management in the fall of 1971.

Greer, Germaine, *The Female Eunuch*. New York: McGraw-Hill, 1971.

Pages 92-131 deal with the avowed mental inferiority of woman and the consequences of this belief are discussed in a chapter on employment and work.

Martin, Wendy, ed., *The American Sisterhood*. New York: Harper & Row, 1972.

An anthology of writings on and by feminists from colonial times to present.

Morgan, Robin, ed., *Sisterhood is Powerful*. New York: Random House, 1970.

A large number of short essays on the liberated woman's views of the oppression she is subjected to within family and society.

Rossi, Alice, "Equality Between the Sexes: An Immodest Proposal," *Daedalus*, vol. 93, no. 2, Spring 1964, pp. 607-52.

Nothing less than a revolutionary change is needed to bring about equality between the sexes. What is called for is the creation of a new social climate in America.

Tanner, Leslie B., *Voices from Women's Liberation*. New York: New American Library, 1970.

A collection of documents presenting the woman's liberation movement from a broad spectrum of viewpoints.

Woman's Role in the Household

Blood, R.O., and Wolfe, "Division of Labor in American Families," in Biddle, B.J., and E.J. Thomas, eds., *Role Theory*. New York: Wiley, 1966.

This article presents a taxonomy of family types insofar as styles in the division of labor within the family is concerned.

Clark, Colin, "The Economics of Housework," *Bulletin of the Oxford Institute of Statistics*, vol. 20, no. 2, May 1958, pp. 205-11.

The exclusion of housework in computations of the GNP "must be considered a purely practical expedient, without theoretical justification." The author proceeds to show how such services could be valued on the basis of costs of similar services produced by institutions and government.

Gilman, Charlotte, "The Waste of Private Housekeeping," *Annals of the American Academy of Political and Social Science*, vol. 48, no. 7, July 1913, pp. 91-95.

This classic note examined efficiency in private housekeeping and pointed up the need for labor-saving equipment in households.

Hamilton, David, *The Consumer in Our Economy*. Boston: Houghton Mifflin, 1962, pp. 32-89.

In these two chapters, Hamilton discusses economic behavior as culture-determined and proceeds to analyze economic wants in terms of cultural factors. The chapters shed light on the decision-making process within the family.

Hedges, J.N., and J. Barnett, "Working Women and the Division of Household Tasks," *Monthly Labor Review*, vol. 95, no. 4, April 1972, pp. 9-14.

More women with children and family responsibilities are now entering the work force. This article deals with the ways in which and the extent to which women with jobs share their household work with other members of their family.

Mandle, Joan, "Women's Liberation: Humanizing Rather Than Polarizing," *Annals of the American Academy of Political and Social Science*, vol. 397, September 1971, pp. 118-28.

Women are conditioned toward home-oriented roles. This conflicts with their acquiring intellectual skills and training and causes women to accept a marginal status in the labor force. The care of families is a crucial task and should not be assigned arbitrarily to women on the basis of an invalid stereotype. Moreover, psychological, social, and economic compensation must be granted for the performance of this function.

Mitchell, Wesley, *The Backward Art of Spending Money*. New York: McGraw-Hill, 1937.

"Despite the importance of the art of spending money, we have developed less skill in its practice than in the practice of making money." The main reason for this backwardness is found to be the need to identify "the values embodied in every housewife's work."

Morgan, James N., et al., *Productive Americans*. Ann Arbor: University of Michigan, 1966.

This report on research conducted at the University of Michigan yields useful insights in the economic behavior of individuals and families. The study seeks to broaden the viewpoint of traditional economics by considering the economics of housework and nonmonetary production.

Myrdal, Alva, and Viola Klein. *Woman's Two Roles: Home and Work*. London: Routledge and Paul, 1962.

An important contribution to knowledge on the role of women in production.

Phelps, Charlotte D., "Is the Household Obsolete?" *The American Economic Review*, vol. 62, no. 2, May 1972, pp. 167-74.

A theory of household formation is developed which helps one to predict the impact of changes in economic conditions on household behavior.

Prest, A.R., and R. Turvey, "Cost-Benefit Analysis: A Survey," *Economic Journal*, vol. 75, no. 4, December 1965, pp. 722-23.

The question of the value of woman's work in the household is raised in connection with cost-benefit analysis of health programs. What is really at issue is how to measure their value not whether to measure it. There are two approaches: either you measure housewives' opportunity cost (a minimum estimate) or replacement cost (a maximum).

Rainwater, Lee, et al., *Workingman's Wife*. New York: Oceana Publications, 1959.

A study in psychology and sociology of the wife's role in working-class households. The book is primarily directed at analyzing tastes and consumption behavior of this rapidly expanding class.

Weisbrod, Burton A., *External Benefits of Public Education: An Economic Analysis*. Princeton: Princeton University Press, 1964.

In his appendix, Weisbrod describes a very ingenious method of measuring the value of a housewife's services, which he views as an increasing function of family size.

Woman's Participation in the Labor Force

Cain, Glen George, *Married Women in the Labor Force: An Economic Analysis*. Chicago: University of Chicago Press, 1966.

A study of the determinants of labor force participation. While more nonwhite women are working, the rate of increase in labor force participation has been slower than for white women as a result of longer education and the availability of welfare programs.

Cohen, Malcolm S., "Participation of Married Women in the Labor Force," *Monthly Labor Review*, vol. 92, no. 10, October 1969, pp. 31-35.

Presents a preliminary description of a labor supply model to assess the impact of such factors as age, education, and age of children on women's labor force participation.

Council of Economic Advisors, "The Economic Role of Women," *Economic Report of the President*. Washington, D.C.: U.S. Government Printing Office, January 1963.

This chapter gives a review of the work patterns for women in the labor force. It also contrasts the age, education, income, and occupational distribution of women with that of men. Also included is a discussion of discrimination and a brief look at government action.

Faim, Paul O., "Persons Not in the Labor Force: Who They Are and Why They Don't Work," *Monthly Labor Review*, vol. 82, no. 7, July 1969, pp. 3-14.

The article reviews the structure of the segment of the population out of the labor force and focuses particularly on nonparticipants who want a job. In analyzing the motives of nonworkers, the author finds that the primary reason invoked is "home responsibilities."

Hayghe, Howard V., "Work Experience of the Population in 1969," *Monthly Labor Review*, vol. 94, no. 1, January 1971, pp. 45-52.

The article dissects some of the trends in the structure of the employed and unemployed work force during the sixties.

Hedges, Janice Neipert, "Women Workers and Manpower Demands in the 1970's," *Monthly Labor Review*, vol. 93, no. 6, June 1970, pp. 19-29.

The article discusses the concentration of women in a few occupations and their absence from some professions and skilled jobs for which there will be significant manpower shortages in the 1970s. A shift of women out of "women's occupations" will have to be effected. The author is optimistic that the necessary attitudinal and institutional changes will take place.

Helfgott, Roy B., "EDP and the Office Work Force," *Industrial and Labor Relations Review*, vol. 19, July 1966, pp. 503-16.

An examination of the consequences of the introduction of electronic data processing in several large offices. By reducing the rate of growth of clerical employment, the computer may also be reducing job opportunities for women.

Loring, Rosalind, and Theodora Wells, *Breakthrough: Women into Management*. New York: Van Nostrand Reinhold, 1972.

This book deals with the American societal and organizational milieu in terms of women in management. Among other things, the authors discuss the problems that have been raised concerning sex-linked stereotypes and give suggestions for affirmative action and affirmative action programs.

Mahoney, Thomas A., "Factors Determining the Labor Force Participation of Married Women," *Industrial and Labor Relations Review*, vol. 14, July 1961, pp. 563-77.

Previous employment experience was found to be the most important predictor of labor force participation of married women. Other factors include age and the presence of children at home. The study is based on a sample of married women in St. Paul, Minnesota.

Myers, George C., "Labor Force Participation of Suburban Mothers," *Journal of Marriage and the Family*, vol. 26, no. 3, March 1964, pp. 306-11.

The study discusses some of the factors found significant in explaining labor force participation of a sample of working mothers of high school students. The type of community and the degree of financial need of family are found relevant.

National Manpower Council, *Womanpower*. New York: Columbia University Press, 1957.

Women constitute a highly significant component of the American labor resources. Their position and performance are discussed as well as the barriers which limit their opportunities and deter the efficient utilization of their potential.

Nye, F. Ivan, and Lois Wladis Hoffman, *The Employed Mother in America*. Chicago: Rand McNally, 1963.

This book contains the results of 19 studies on the employed mother in America. Numerous questions are treated including the effect on children, the familial adjustment necessary, the performance of the working mother.

Oppenheimer, Valerie K., "The Interaction of Demand and Supply and Its Effect on the Female Labor Force in the United States," *Population Studies*, vol. 21, no. 3, 1967, pp. 239-59.

One of the more salient features of the change in the structure of the female labor force in the U.S. is the relative increase of mature married women participation as compared with single younger women.

Perrella, Vera C., "Women and the Labor Force," *Monthly Labor Review*, vol. 91, no. 2, February 1968, pp. 1-12.

The structure and change of the female labor force are considered. The study points to the continued increase in married women participation as the major factor of change.

Sandell, Steven H., "Economic Equality for Women—Discussion," *The American Economic Review*, vol. 62, no. 2, May 1972, pp. 175-76.

Much of the observed occupational distribution differences between men and women can be attributed to different expected lengths of labor market involvement and different incentives to invest in human capital for the sexes.

Shiffman, Jacob, "Marital and Family Characteristics of Workers, March 1960," *Monthly Labor Review*, vol. 84, no. 4, April 1961, pp. 355-64.

The article describes some of the more important changes in labor force participation of various groups classified according to family and marital status.

Smuts, Robert W., *Women and Work in America*. New York: Columbia University Press, 1959.

While women's labor force participation rate continues to rise, numerous cultural barriers still block the entrance of women in specific occupations and in the labor force in general. These obstacles reflect a "cultural lag" which will soon be overcome.

"A Symposium: Women in the Labor Force," *Industrial Relations*, vol. 7, no. 3, May 1968, pp. 187-248.

Margaret S. Gordon's introduction focuses on the impact of early marriage and childbearing on woman's opportunities. Eli Ginzberg laments the lack of concern on the part of economists for problems that do not fit their models and proceeds to suggest three policy areas on which we must concentrate: the family, rather than the individual, has to be viewed as the basic unit of employment, child care centers must be provided, and the lack of unionization and low wage levels of women's occupations must be remedied. Gertrude McNally draws a sweeping picture of the patterns and problems of women's employment. Finally, Harold Wilensky's article reviews the obstacles which hinder woman's entry in the labor force and her choice of occupation.

U.S. Department of Labor, Women's Bureau. *Who Are the Working Mothers?* Leaflet 37, May 1970.

A statistical study of employed mothers in America. The data demonstrate that most mothers are working for financial reasons.

U.S. Department of Labor, Women's Bureau. *Why Women Work.* 1970.

A short statistical overview of the patterns of female labor force participation in the U.S. Most women are found to work out of need.

Waldman, Elizabeth, "Changes in the Labor Force Activity of Women," *Monthly Labor Review*, vol. 93, no. 6, June 1970, pp. 18-27.

The author examines the many-faceted consequences of the increase in the labor force participation of married women which accounted, in 1968-69, for half the increase in workers.

Waldman, Elizabeth, "Marital and Family Characteristics of the Labor Force," *Monthly Labor Review*, vol. 93, no. 5, May 1970, pp. 18-27.

This report points to an increasing proportion of young married women in the 1969 labor force.

Waldman, Elizabeth, and Anne M. Young, "Marital and Family Charcteristics of Workers, March 1970," *Monthly Labor Review*, vol. 94, no. 3, March 1971, pp. 46-50.

In 1970 again, married women led the annual rise in the U.S. labor force. Data on unemployment by race and sex are also presented.

Weisskoff, Francine Blau, "Women's Place in the Labor Market," *The American Economic Review*, vol. 62, no. 2, May 1972, pp. 161-66.

This is a summarization of the trends in women's involvement in market work and their employment status. The persistence of occupational segregation in the labor market by sex is the main obstacle to the attainment of economic equality for women.

Wells, Jean A., "Women College Graduates 7 Years Later," *Monthly Labor Review*, vol. 90, no. 7, July 1967, pp. 28-32.

Presents the results of a resurvey of women graduates 7 years after graduation. A Women's Bureau study.

Employment and Earnings

Arnott, Catherine C., "Husbands' Attitudes and Wives' Commitments to Employment," *Journal of Marriage and the Family*, vol. 34, November 1972, pp. 673-83.

Shared husband-wife role preference leads to role continuity or role change, depending on whether their shared preference is for the wife's present role or a different one. In general women with liberal perceptions of autonomy expect their husbands to make more adjustments than themselves. Those with conservative attitudes are more willing to make the adjustments themselves. This relationship did not hold up when women were in occupational roles that their husbands opposed.

Astin, Helen S., et al., *Women: A Bibliography on Their Education and Career*. Washington: Human Service Press, 1971.

Items 101-212 deal with woman's work.

Baker, Elizabeth F., *Technology and Woman's Work*. New York: Columbia University Press, 1964.

The author considers the impact of technological change on employment opportunities for women in the last 150 years. The barriers to occupational mobility into traditionally men-dominated jobs are also examined.

Bernard, Jessie, *Academic Women*. University Park: Pennsylvania University Press, 1964.

A major study of the contribution of women to "the total academic enterprise in the United States." Chapter 3 deals with discrimination, chapter 5 with differences between academic men and women. The appendixes contain the results of several studies.

Business and Professional Women's Foundation. *Women Executives: A Selected Annotated Bibliography*. Washington: Business and Professional Women's Foundation, 1970.

Cohen, Malcolm S., "Sex Differences in Compensation," *Journal of Human Resources*, vol. 6, no. 4, Fall 1971, pp. 434-47.

A test of various hypotheses explaining differences in pay between men and women. Discrimination is not found significant. The clustering of women in lower-paying jobs is the most important factor though differences in qualifications, seniority, fringe benefits, and working conditions are also relevant.

Dodge, Norton T., *Women in the Soviet Economy*. Baltimore: John Hopkins, 1966.

A statistical profile of woman's employment and education in the Soviet Union. The study focuses particularly on women in the professions and in science.

Epstein, Cynthia Fuchs, *Women's Place: Options and Limits in Professional Careers*. Berkeley: University of California Press, 1970.

The author analyzes the institutions and mores which conspire to limit women's success. Why women tend to settle at the bottom of the occupational ladder is the basic question she addresses. An extensive bibliography on professional women is included.

Feilke, M.F., "Women, Women Everywhere But Not a Manager in Sight," *Iron Age*, August 27, 1970, pp. 63-65.

Tomorrow's shortage of managers will accelerate the penetration by women of the executive world. Women have numerous qualities that make them extremely effective managers. Prejudice and preconceptions on the role of woman must still be overcome. A first step could be acceptance by top management of a policy of equal opportunity.

Ferriss, Abbott, L., *Indicators of Trends in the Status of American Women*. New York: Russell Sage Foundation, 1971.

A vast array of trend data are presented on education, marital status, employment and income, health and leisure. The author finds no reason in the objective status of women for the recent interest in women's liberation.

Fogarty, Michael P., et al., *Sex, Career and Family*. London: Allen & Unwin, 1971.

An extensive study of the reasons there are so few women in top jobs. The Enquiry's findings include the propositions that high-level careers for women are "practicable and desirable" and that positive action is needed aimed primarily at adapting employment practices to women's needs.

Fogarty, Michael, et al., *Women in Top Jobs*. London: Allen & Unwin, 1971.

Presents in detail the results of four surveys of opinion of women in top jobs in government and business.

Fuchs, Victor R., "Differences in Hourly Earnings Between Men and Women," *Monthly Labor Review*, vol. 94, no. 5, May 1971.

The study is based on the one-in-one-thousand sample of the 1960 Census of Population and Housing. The differential in hourly earnings of men and women is large. It can be explained primarily in terms of "the different roles assigned to men and women" which in turn affect choice of occupation, labor force attachment, location of work, and other such variables. Employer discrimination is not a direct influence on earnings but it does affect role differentiation.

Ginsberg, Eli, and Alice M. Yohalem, *Educated Women: Self Portraits*. New York: Columbia University Press, 1966.

A series of self-portraits of women, classifed in four broad types according to their life styles.

Gross, Edward, "Plus Ça Change . . . The Sexual Structure of Occupations Over Time," *Social Problems*, vol. 16, no. 2, Fall 1968, pp. 198-208.

A modified Duncan's Index shows no apparent change in the degree of occupational segregation, while through a measure derived by Gibbs, some improvement is demonstrated. This reduction may be due more to men entering female occupations than to the reverse.

Hauser, Philip M., "Labor Force," in Robert E.L. Farris, ed., *Handbook of Modern Sociology*. Chicago: Rand McNally, 1964, chapter 5.

The point is made in this article that the increase in women's participation in the labor force can hardly be regarded as a spectacular accomplishment: they have tended to displace younger and older age groups.

Hooks, Janet M., *Women's Occupations Through Seven Decades*. Washington: U.S. Government Printing Office, 1948.

A well-known discussion of woman's place in industrial society.

Hoskins, Dalmer, and Lenore E. Bixby, *Women and Social Security: Law and Policy in Five Countries*. Research Report No. 42, Social Security Administration, U.S. Department of Health, Education, and Welfare. Washington, D.C.: Government Printing Office, 1973.

This booklet describes the social insurance programs as they affect women in Belgium, Germany, France, Great Britain, and the United States.

Hughes, Marija Matich, *The Sexual Barrier: Legal and Economic Aspects of Employment*. Berkeley: University of California Hastings College of Law, 1970.

An annotated bibliography covering the period 1959 to 1970 is included. The topics covered are the law, discrimination, pay differentials, and professional opportunities for women.

Koontz, Elizabeth, "The Women's Bureau Looks at the Future," *Monthly Labor Review*, vol. 93, no. 6, June 1970, pp. 3-9.

The article which introduces a special section on women at work, focuses on the changes in the Women's Bureau's functions and objectives over the last 50 years.

Kreps, Juanita, *Sex in the Marketplace*. Baltimore: John Hopkins, 1971.

A penetrating analysis of the factors to be considered in the analysis of women's employment and earnings. The author focuses on the literature and, in view of its paucity, enunciates some of the questions yet unanswered. She examines at length the supply and demand forces which account for the concentration of women in selected occupations and their acceptance of lower pay. She concludes that more must be learned about the opportunity cost of woman's participation in the market (the value of nonmarket work) and about the structural and institutional system by which women are excluded from certain occupations. A bibliography is included.

Larsen, C.A., "Equal Pay for Women in the United Kingdom," *International Labor Review*, vol. 103, no. 1, January 1971, pp. 1-11.

Analyzes the likely impact of the Equal Pay Act of 1970 which requires companies to remove all discrimination against women by 1975. Equal pay, far from fostering unemployment, may widen women's opportunities by contributing to the removal of the attitude that woman's labor is inferior.

McNulty, Donald J., "Differences in Pay Between Men and Women Workers," *Monthly Labor Review*, vol. 90, no. 12, December 1967, pp. 40-43.

Suggests that discriminatory practices are not a major factor contributing to wage differentials between men and women. When comparisons are made as between men and women in single establishments, differences are small and can be explained in terms of such factors as seniority and excessive broadness of occupational classes.

Miller, Frank B., and Mary Ann Coghill, "Sex and the Personnel Manager," *Industrial and Labor Relations Review*, vol. 18, October 1964, pp. 32-44.

Women have played a very significant role in personnel work as long as such work was primarily welfare oriented. The shift toward technicism in personnel work has resulted in a decline in women's participation.

Oaxaca, Ronald, "Male-Female Wage Differentials in Urban Labor Markets." Unpublished paper.

An extensive econometric treatment of wage differentials based on data from the 1967 Survey of Economic Opportunity. Sex discrimination accounts for the major portion of the pay differences between men and women, especially among black workers.

Oppenheimer, Valerie K., *The Female Labor Force in the United States*. Berkeley: University of California Press, 1970. Population Monograph Series No. 5.

This work is based on the writer's Ph.D. dissertation. It is a major study of woman's participation in the labor force and of the market factors that result in her segregation in specific occupations.

Peterson, Esther, "Working Women," *Daedalus*, vol. 93, no. 2, Spring 1964, pp. 671-99.

A factual statement of the employment of women in the early sixties. The pattern of employment of women is infinitely complex and not commonly understood. One of the more serious problems is the existence of a differential in pay for equal work done by men and women.

Report of the President's Commission on the Status of Women, *American Women*. Washington: U.S. Government Printing Office, 1963.

The report surveys women's position in the United States and suggests recommendations for future action.

Sanborn, Henry, "Pay Differences Between Men and Women," *Industrial and Labor Relations Review*, vol. 17, no. 4, July 1964, pp. 534-50.

The author describes pay differences between men and women and studies the extent and nature of pay discrimination. The conclusion is that discrimination is significant but it is affected more by consumers and coworkers than by employers.

Simchak, Morag MacLeod, "Equal Pay in the United States," *International Labor Review*, vol. 103, no. 6, June 1971, pp. 541-58.

There are grounds for optimism in the recent narrowing of the earnings gap. The main factor has been the recent legislation.

Simon, Rita James, et al., "The Woman Ph.D.: A Recent Profile," *Social Problems*, vol. 15, no. 2, Fall 1967, pp. 221-35.

A descriptive study of the professional characteristics of women who have received their Ph.D. in four areas between 1958 and 1963. Differences between men and women in employment conditions and productivity are found to be relatively small.

Spiegel, Jeanne, *Working Mothers: A Selected Annotated Bibliography*. Business and Professional Women's Foundation, 1968.

Suelzle, Marijean, "Women in Labor," *Transaction*, vol. 8, nos. 1-2, 1970, pp. 50-58.

Despite popular myths to the contrary, women's status in the economy has been worsening in the last half century. Both occupational and wealth data are presented.

Thorsell, Siv, "Employer Attitudes to Female Employees," in Edmund Dahlstrom, ed., *The Changing Roles of Men and Women*. Boston: Beacon Press, 1971, pp. 135-69.

A study conducted in Sweden presented a detailed picture of the patterns of occupational segregation in industry. Firms appeared to benefit from sexual segregation because the wage level was lower in occupations where women were concentrated.

U.S. Department of Labor, Women's Bureau, *Automation and Women Workers*. 1970.

It is difficult to measure the impact of technological change on occupational opportunities for women. Numerous other factors also played a role in expanding opportunities for women in the 1960s.

U.S. Department of Labor, Women's Bureau, *Background Facts on Women Workers in the United States*. Washington: U.S. Government Printing Office, 1970.

Data on female labor force participation, occupations, unemployment, and earnings.

U.S. Department of Labor, Women's Bureau, *Economic Indicators Relating to Equal Pay, 1963*. Pamphlet 9, 1963.

A statistical study of pay differentials between men and women in similar occupations in business and government. Significant differences are found in all areas except the federal government.

U.S. Department of Labor, Women's Bureau, *Fact Sheet on the Earnings Gap*. 1970.

This pamphlet includes figures on median and average wages of women and men. The differential in pay is found to be considerable and to have increased in recent years.

U.S. Department of Labor, Women's Bureau, *1969 Handbook on Women Workers*. Bulletin 294, 1969.

A useful statistical profile of women's employment and earnings.

U.S. Department of Labor, Women's Bureau, *Negro Women*. Washington: U.S. Government Printing Office, 1968.

A statistical profile of the status and employment opportunities of black women in the U.S.

U.S. Department of Labor, Women's Bureau, *Women in the Federal Service, 1939-1959.* Washington: U.S. Government Printing Office, 1961.

A statistical profile of the occupations and status of women in the federal government.

Vangsnes, Kari, "Equal Pay in Norway," *International Labor Review*, vol. 103, no. 4, April 1971, pp. 379-92.

Considerable pay differences still exist between men and women despite the 1961 Agreement between workers' and employers' unions. These differences are due to the concentration of women in low-pay occupations, differences in job description, age composition, education, and training, and the tendency for discontinuity in female employment.

Wallace, Phyllis A., "The Role of Women in Management," Unpublished paper, Metropolitan Applied Research Corporation, New York, August 1971.

Income data show that black males follow white males in average earnings. White women rank below black men, while black women rank last among the four groups. In periods of change in employment policy, black women may be able to outrank white women in economic progress because they are both black and female.

Occupational Choice

Almquist, Elizabeth, and Shirley S. Angrist, "Career Salience and Atypicality of Occupational Choice Among College Women," *Journal of Marriage and the Family*, vol. 32, no. 2, 1970, pp. 242-49.

A test of the "deviance hypothesis" as a predictor of women's participation in men-dominated occupations. The findings reveal that career-oriented women are not significantly different in terms of background and values.

Angrist, Shirley S., "Variations in Women's Adult Aspirations During College," *Journal of Marriage and the Family*, vol. 34, August 1972, pp. 465-68.

Five types of students are discussed: the careerist, the noncareerist, the convert, the defector, and the shifter. Only the careerist consistently plans her future life around both family and occupation.

Astin, Helen S., "Career Development of Girls During the High School Years," *Journal of Counseling Psychology*, vol. 15, no. 6, June 1968, pp. 536-40.

The study seeks to relate career plans of high school senior girls to the type of high schools attended and various background factors.

Astin, Helen S., "Stability and Change in the Career Plans of Ninth-Grade Girls," *Personnel and Guidance Journal*, vol. 46, no. 10, October 1968, pp. 961-66.

This study reveals that changes in career plans during high school occur as a result of a reappraisal of opportunities and increasing self-awareness. The findings are derived from the analysis of a sample of 7061 girls from the Project TALENT Data Bank.

Bailyn, Lotte, "Notes on the Role of Choice in the Psychology of Professional Women," *Daedalus*, vol. 93, no. 2, Spring 1964, pp. 700-10.

There is a great need for research in the social and psychological variables involved when getting work is not a question of necessity but one of choice—as is the case for the educated housewife.

Blau, Peter, et al., "Occupational Choice—A Conceptual Framework," *Industrial and Labor Relations Review*, vol. 9, no. 4, July 1956, pp. 531-43.

The authors present a conceptual scheme to classify factors explaining why people end up in different occupations. Occupational entry is determined by a choice process and a selection process, both of which are influenced by the social structure.

Eyde, Lorraine D., "Work Motivation of Women College Graduates: Five-Year Follow-Up," *Journal of Counseling Psychology*, vol. 15, no. 2, 1968, pp. 199-202.

A study of the stability of women's commitment to paid occupations and of their motives for working outside the home.

Eyde, Lorraine D., *Work Values and Background Factors as Predictors of Women's Desire to Work*. Columbus, Ohio: Ohio State University, 1962.

Assesses the impact of work values, attitudes, and background on women's work motivation. The results were based on surveys of a group of college seniors and a group of alumnae.

Farmer, Helen S., and Martin J. Bohn, Jr., "Home-Career Conflict Reduction and the Level of Career Interest in Women," *Journal of Counseling Psychology*, vol. 17, no. 3, 1970, pp. 228-32.

If home-career conflict is reduced, the level of vocational interest is raised among women, whether they are single or married.

Faunce, Patricia Spencer, "Personality Characteristics and Vocational Interests Related to the College Persistence of Academically Gifted Women," *Journal of Counseling Psychology*, vol. 15, no. 1, January 1968, pp. 31-40.

Those women who persisted through college to graduation had significantly different personality structures (more insightful, more modest, free from inner tensions) and vocational interests (as revealed by SVIB scores).

Harmon, Lenore W., "Anatomy of Career Commitment in Women," *Journal of Counseling Psychology*, vol. 17, no. 1, January 1970, pp. 77-80.

No significant differences in career plans at age 18 or levels of satisfaction in home life at age 33 was found as between women with strong career commitments and non-career-committed women. The former group, however, is shown to stay longer in college and work more outside the home.

Harmon, Lenore W., "The Childhood and Adolescent Career Plans of College Women," *Journal of Vocational Behavior*, vol. 1, no. 1, January 1971, pp. 45-56.

The author suggests that vocational counselors should encourage unusual occupational preferences common among preadolescents but absent in their later years when women turn to more conventional feminine fields.

Horner, Matina S., "Fail: Bright Women," *Psychology Today*, vol. 3, no. 6, November 1969, pp. 36-41.

A study of the determinants of motivation for achievement. Anticipation of success (especially success over a man) can provoke anxiety. Success is thereby inhibited.

Keniston, Elen and Kenneth, "An American Anachronism: The Image of Women and Work," *The American Scholar*, vol. 33, no. 3, Summer 1964, pp. 355-75.

The prevailing definition of the good life for women is totally outmoded. The conception that marriage and family can fulfill all emotional and intellectual needs of women is a fantasy in our age, but the persistence of this fantasy leads to ambivalence and guilt and hinders the process of rationally choosing a career.

Masih, Lalit K., "Career Saliency and Its Relation to Certain Needs, Interests and Job Values," *Personnel and Guidance Journal*, vol. 45, no. 7, July 1967, pp. 653-58.

Women are less career-oriented than men. Individuals with high career saliency are shown to seek achievement and fame. The tests are based on a sample of college juniors and seniors.

Parrish, John B., "Professional Womanpower as a National Resource," *Quarterly Review of Economics and Business*, vol. 1, no. 1, Spring 1961, pp. 54-63.

Participation of women in the nation's intellectual labor force has declined in terms of men's and barely kept up with population growth since the thirties. The causes are earlier marriage, higher rate of family formation, and women's preferences for low-skill jobs. This last factor is attributed to the rising costs of higher education and the increasing attractiveness of early home formation.

Perucci, Carolyn Commings, "Minority Status and the Pursuit of Professional Careers of Women in Science and Engineering," *Social Forces*, vol. 49, no. 2, 1970, pp. 245-58.

Men and women trained as scientists and engineers obtain similar work after graduation. A differential in pay and job level appears early and increases over time. The traditional explanation that women value income and prestige less than men is shown to be unfounded.

Rose, Arnold M., "The Adequacy of Women's Expectations for Adult Roles," *Social Forces*, vol. 30, no. 1, October 1951, pp. 69-77.

One of the main reasons for woman's lack of success is that her advance expectations about future roles tend to be indefinite, inconsistent, and unrealistic. Inadequate expectations, in turn, result from the haziness of woman's role in industrial society.

Rossi, Alice S., "Women in Science: Why So Few?" *Science*, vol. 148, May 1965, pp. 1196-202.

Various social and psychological obstacles restrict women's choice and pursuit of careers in science: the priority of marriage in women's aspirations, out-of-date views on the undesirable impact of maternal employment on children, early family influences, and social norms which hinder the development of certain intellectual abilities in girls.

Shea, John R., Roger D. Roderick, Frederick A. Zeller, and Andrew I. Kohen, *Years for Decision: A Longitudinal Study of the Educational and Labor*

Market Experience of Young Women. Columbus, Ohio: Ohio State University, Center for Human Resource Research, 1971.

The preliminary report on a major five-year study of the education and experience of young women and their career choice. Some emphasis is placed on comparing employment behavior of white and black women.

U.S. Department of Labor, Women's Bureau. *Expanding Opportunities for Girls: Their Special Counseling Needs*. 1970.

Inadequate career aspirations among girls is a major factor explaining their low achievement. Better counseling is called for.

Wallace, Jacquelyn L., and Thelma H. Leonard, "Factors Affecting Vocational and Educational Decision-Making of High School Girls," *Journal of Home Economics*, vol. 63, no. 4, April 1971, pp. 241-45.

A survey of girls in 509 public schools in Louisiana indicated a strong relationship between aspirations and expectation levels. One finding is that girls who expected to drop out of high school were not trained to enter the labor market.

Williamson, Thomas R., and Edward J. Karras, "Job Satisfaction Variables Among Female Clerical Workers," *Journal of Applied Psychology*, vol. 54, no. 4, April 1970, pp. 343-46.

Female clerical workers are more concerned with the job environment than with self-fulfillment in their job. Men, on the contrary, pay less attention to "hygienes," but seek a job that motivates them highly.

Selection Procedures and Sex Differences in Productivity

Anastasi, A., *Differential Psychology*. New York: Macmillan, 1958, 3rd ed.

Chapter 14 deals with sex differences. The author reviews the various studies of sex differences and their biological and cultural determinants. The conclusion is that one cannot speak of "superiority or inferiority, but only of specific differences in aptitudes or personality." These differences are primarily the result of cultural factors and are so overlapping within each person that one cannot use group stereotypes to compare individual men and women. A bibliography containing 150 items is appended.

Anderson, D., and C.S. Pearson, "Changing Sex Requirements in Michigan Class Specification," *Public Personnel Review*, vol. 28, no. 3, March 1967, pp. 153-55.

The new guidelines used by the state of Michigan in establishing sex restrictions in employment are spelled out in this short article.

Anderson, Betty R., and Martha P. Rogers, ed., *Personnel Testing and Equal Employment Opportunity*. Washington: U.S. Government Printing Office, December 1970.

Questions the fairness of many ability tests as a basis for hiring, screening, and promoting and suggests some guidelines to improve testing. The emphasis is on inadvertent discrimination.

Ash, Philip, "Discrimination in Hiring and Placement," *Personnel*, vol. 44, no. 6, November/December 1967, pp. 8-17.

Discusses the impact of the Civil Rights Act on personnel selection procedure and emerging trends that may influence this process.

Bernard, Jessie, "The Public Interest and the Sexual Division of Labor," *Women and the Public Interest*. Chicago: Aldine, 1971, pp. 103-35.

Female occupational segregation is a universal phenomenon but occupations reserved for women differ in various societies. No matter how occupations are divided by sex, whatever men do has more prestige than what women do. College-trained women are now more likely to be employed and their number are increasing. But they are taking lower positions than in the past. One aspect of sexism is the feeling that women should succeed in male occupations in order to be judged truly successful.

Brown, D.G., "Sex-Role Development in a Changing Culture," *Psychological Bulletin*, vol. 55, no. 4, April 1958, pp. 232-43.

The author concludes that sex roles are converging in modern society. The article is based on a survey of the literature on sex roles perception.

Goldberg, Philip, "Are Women Prejudiced Against Women?" *Transaction*, vol. 5, no. 5, April 1968, pp. 28-31.

On the basis of a sample of 140 college girls, the author finds that, even when the work is identical, women value the professional work of men more highly than that of women. This is found to apply even in fields traditionally reserved for women (nursing, dietetics). The author rationalizes his results with the proposition that prejudice distorts perception of performance.

Isambert-Jamati, Viviane, "Absenteeism Among Women Workers in Industry," *International Labor Review*, vol. 85, no. 3, March 1962, pp. 248-61.

The higher rate of absenteeism among women is due neither to physiological or psychological differences (between men and women), nor to the burdens of householding. The concentration of women in lower-scale occupations is the single most important factor.

Kirkwood, John H., "To Test or Not to Test," *Personnel*, vol. 44, no. 6, November/December 1967, pp. 18-26.

The role of psychological testing is being reevaluated in the light of experience under the Civil Rights Act and recent court decisions.

Goodall, Kenneth, "Tie Line," *Psychology Today*, vol. 5, no. 7, December 1971, pp. 36-38.

Goodall reports on two research projects which have not yet resulted in publication. Teresa Levitin, University of Michigan, found that although discrimination is widespread, women fail to perceive it. The Johnson O'Connor Company has administered vocational and aptitude tests to some

330,000 persons. The results, unprocessed, will yield, useful insights in sexual differences in aptitudes.

Maccoby, Eleanor E., ed., *The Development of Sex Differences*. Stanford, California: Stanford University Press, 1966.

The book contains the results of discussions on sex differences held at Stanford University.

McKiever, M.F., *The Health of Women Who Work*. Public Health Service Publication No. 1314. Washington: U.S. Department of Health, Education and Welfare, 1965.

The booklet provides information on numerous questions regarding health and employment. Specific findings are also presented on a comparison between male and female health. Women are found to have fewer heart attacks, live longer, and be less subject to disease; they average a slightly larger number of sick days per year.

Oetzel, Roberta M., "Annotated Bibliography of Research Studies on Sex Differences," Maccoby, Eleanor E., ed., *The Development of Sex Differences*, 1966.

The period of some 30 years of studies is covered in this extensive bibliography.

Oppenheimer, Valerie K., "The Sex Labeling of Jobs," *Industrial Relations*, vol. 7, no. 3, May 1968, pp. 219-34.

A study of female-dominated occupations such as teaching, nursing, and secretarial work. The author analyzes the characteristics of jobs which make them suitable for women.

Schwartz, Eleanor Brantley, "The Sex Barrier in Business," *Atlanta Economic Review*, vol. 21, no. 6, March/June 1971, pp. 4-9.

A survey of opinions of 300 executives of large businesses, 300 executives from small firms, and 300 women executives. In the sample women constitute only 2 percent of senior management (1 percent in big business). Male executives are generally pleased with the performance of female managers. A majority believe that investment in training of women does not provide as high a return as investment in men, and that women are less career motivated. Female executives would prefer working for a man.

Tyler, Leona, *The Psychology of Human Differences*. New York: Appleton-Century Crofts, 1965.

An excellent textbook in the field of group differences. Chapter 10 deals with sex differences and stresses the point that high achievement is rare among women even though girls succeed in school.

U.S. Department of Labor, Women's Bureau, *Facts About Women's Absenteeism and Labor Turnover*, 1969.

Sex is not a good predictor of job performance. The skill-level of jobs, the worker's seniority, and his age explain most of the variation in absenteeism and turnover among workers.

U.S. Department of Labor, Women's Bureau, *Sex Discrimination in Employment Practices*, 1968.

The report of a joint Conference of the University of California Extension Service, the Personnel and Industrial Relations Association, Inc., and the Women's Bureau. Discrimination against women is still widespread in public and private employment.

Discrimination

Bergmann, Barbara R., "Occupational Segregation, Wages and Profits When Employers Discriminate by Race or Sex," *Journal of Political Economy*, vol. 79, no. 2, March/April 1971.

The author introduces a simple model to show the relationship between wage differentials and occupational segregation. Basic marginal productivity theory is used to study the impact of discrimination on profit. The conclusion is that in certain circumstances, and especially when the target group is not excessively large or small, discrimination will significantly raise profits.

Bergmann, Barbara R. "The Economics of Women's Liberation," a paper presented at the Annual Meeting of the American Psychological Association. Washington: 1971.

Highlights the division of labor within the nuclear family as an impediment to equal employment opportunity for women.

Bird, Caroline, "Women in Business: The Invisible Bar," *Personnel*, May/June 1968, pp. 29-35.

The invisible bar that keeps women down is the assumption that women cannot be serious about a vocation. Some institutional barriers are noted which reflect this attitude: aggressiveness on the part of women arouses antagonism, access to information is denied her, she lacks bargaining power, her judgment is not trusted, she has no "wife" to turn to for approval.

Bird, Caroline, and Sara Welles Briller, *Born Female: The High Cost of Keeping Women Down*. New York: McKay, 1968.

Women's talents and abilities are being wasted and destroyed by excessive discrimination. Rare are the women who succeed to surmount the numerous obstacles that are placed by society on their paths to success. A classic in the field.

Brimmer, A.F., and H. Harper, "Economists' Perception of Minority Economic Problems: A View of the Emerging Literature," *Journal of Economic Literature*, vol. 8, no. 3, September 1970, pp. 783-805.

Poverty and minority problems received only limited attention from economists during the sixties. The article surveys journal literature on the subject and contains an extensive bibliography on such topics as discrimination and employment problems of minorities.

Chabaud, Jacqueline, "Still Too Rarely Possible: A Real Skilled Occupation," *The Education and Advancement of Women*. Paris: UNESCO, 1970, pp. 57-76.

One of the interesting points made in this article is that the feminization of a profession deters the entry of men. Hence, too many women should not be hired to solve the world's shortage of primary school teachers. The best training and occupations are reserved for men the world over.

Fidell, L.S., "Empirical Verification of Sex Discrimination in Hiring Practices in Psychology," *American Psychologist*, vol. 25, no. 12, December 1970, pp. 1094-98.

On the basis of a study of 155 departments of psychology, the author concludes that sex is a factor in the determination of position and rank offered to applicants.

Hahn, Marilyn C., "Equal Rights for Women in Career Development," *Personnel*, July/August 1970, pp. 55-59.

An optimistic description of the forces tending to foster equal rights for women in employment. Although "full integration will mean changing deeply-rooted ideas about sexual roles," a great deal is being accomplished as a result of positive legislation, democratization of business organizational structure, and technological change.

Jacobson, Carolyn J., "Some Special Problems the Older Woman Encounters When Seeking Employment," *Industrial and Labor Relations Forum*, vol. 7, no. 3, October 1971, pp. 66-75.

Despite recent legislation, women workers 35 and over face severe discrimination by employers.

James, Ralph C., "Discrimination Among Women in Bombay Textiles," *Industrial and Labor Relations Review*, vol. 15, January 1962, pp. 209-20.

In contrast with most western countries where discrimination in industry has decreased steadily in recent years, discrimination in India's major urban industry has been increasing.

Klein, Viola, *Britain's Married Women Workers*. New York: Humanities Press, 1965.

The results of two surveys. First, public attitudes towards women working outside their homes and the experience of working wives; second, employers' attitudes and practices regarding married women workers. The most significant findings are that, on the one hand, productive work has now become not a burden, but a condition for self-fulfillment for the married woman; on the other, employers are still reticent to employ married women and do so merely as a temporary expedient in periods of labor shortage.

Kresge, Pat, "The Human Dimensions of Sex Discrimination," *Journal of the American Association of University Women*, vol. 64, no. 2, February 1970, pp. 6-9.

This article reproduces the results of an opinion survey on the status of women. A significant percentage of the respondents cited instances of sex discrimination to which they have been subjected.

McCune, Shirley, "Thousands Reply to Opinionaire: Many Documented Cases of Sex Discrimination," *Journal of the American Association of University Women*, vol. 64, no. 5, May 1970, pp. 202-6.

This, too, shows the results of a survey of opinion. It contains a summary of responses by 4065 women and 2940 men.

Mancke, Richard B., "Lower Pay For Women: A Case of Economic Discrimination?" *Industrial Relations*, vol. 10, no. 3, October 1971, pp. 316-26.

Women are not victims of economic discrimination based on sex. An alternative hypothesis to explain the lower wages for women is tested and validated in this article: "Employers believe that, on the average, the probability of turnover is much higher for women than it is for men."

Mancke, Richard B., "Lower Pay for Women: A Case of Economic Discrimination: Reply," *Industrial Relations*, vol. 11, no. 2, pp. 285-88.

Mancke responds to an article by Myra Strober in terms of an article written by Mancke in 1971 (see references to original Mancke article and Strober's reply).

May, John W., Jr., "Every Day is Ladies' Day," *Public Service: The Human Side of Government*. Harper & Row, 1971, pp. 83-93.

We must use women workers better. The percentage of post-graduate degrees granted to women has fallen in the 1960s as compared with the 1930s. In 1961, the President's Commission on the status of women revealed that federal agencies were permitted to restrict certain positions on the basis of sex.

Morse, Dean, *The Peripheral Worker*. New York: Columbia University Press, 1969.

Pages 129-48 in particular deal with women's position on the periphery of the work force.

Phelps, Edmund S., "The Statistical Theory of Racism and Sexism," *The American Economic Review*, vol. 62, no. 2, September 1972, pp. 659-61.

Statistical formulae are based on the belief that an employer who seeks to maximize expected profit will discriminate against blacks or women if he believes that they are less qualified, less reliable, or less long-term than whites or men and if the cost of gaining information about the individual applicants is excessive.

"Resolutions on the Status of Women," *American Quarterly*, vol. 24, no. 4, October 1972, pp. 550-54.

A list of resolutions are given which concern the removal of discriminatory practices against women. This list was approved by the Council of the American Studies Association in April of 1972.

Strober, Myra H., "Lower Pay for Women: A Case of Economic Discrimination?" *Industrial Relations*, vol. 11, no. 2, May 1972, pp. 279-84.

The author is responding to an article by the same name which appeared in the October 1971 issue of *Industrial Relations* by Richard Mancke. She argues against Mancke's turnover hypothesis and training hypothesis.

U.S. House of Representatives, Hearings Before Subcommittee No. 4 of the
Committee on the Judiciary, *Equal Rights for Men and Women 1971*. 92nd
Congress, 1st Session, 1971. Washington: U.S. Government Printing Office,
1971.

A collection of testimony on various relevant topics.

White, Martha S., "Psychological and Social Barriers to Women in Science,"
Science, vol. 170, October 1970, pp. 413-16.

Women are denied the benefits of interaction with colleagues in science,
especially if they have experienced interrupted careers.

Zeller, Harriet, "Discrimination Against Women, Occupational Segregation, and
the Relative Wage," *The American Economic Review*, vol. 62, no. 2, May
1972, pp. 157-60.

Discrimination against women in male-dominated occupations plays a
central role in explaining occupational segregation and low relative wage. An
increase in the demand for women in masculine occupations is dependent
upon their having gotten into these occupations in the first place. A
decreasing relative wage won't accomplish this.

Women and Labor Unions

Boone, Gladys, *The Women's Trade Union Leagues in Great Britain and the
U.S.A.* New York: Columbia University Press, 1942.

In this book, Gladys Boone traces the history of the women's trade union
leagues in the U.S. and Great Britain. These institutions are examined by the
author in relation to both the labor and the feminist movements.

Cook, Alice H., "Women and American Trade Unions," *Annals of the American
Academy of Political and Social Science*, vol. 375, no. 1, January 1968,
pp. 124-32.

Women's participation in trade unions is examined. The author finds that
even when women constitute the majority, they are assigned and accept the
status of a minority. Few changes in attitudes and practices were found to
characterize the 1960s as compared with previous periods. Previous articles
on the same subject were written by Theresa Wolfson (May 1929) and Gladys
Dickison (May 1947). This article is included in a special section of the
Annals entitled "Women Around the World." Other articles deal with the
political and legal status of women, their place in the economy, their
education, and the goals yet to be achieved.

Dowey, Lucretia M., "Women in Labor Unions," *Monthly Labor Review*, vol.
94, no. 2, February 1971, pp. 42-48.

The increase in the number of women in unions has not kept pace with the
growth of the female labor force (1958-68). Various reasons are presented.
Only few women hold offices in international unions and the situation shows
no sign of improving.

Goldstein, Mark L., "Blue-Collar Women and American Labor Unions," *Industrial and Labor Relations Forum*, vol. 7, no. 3, October 1971, pp. 1-35.

Traces the history and problems of the blue-collar female worker. Many forms of discrimination—by employers, unions, and fellow workers—have effectively barred women from high-paying positions.

Henry, Alice, *The Trade Union Woman*. New York: D. Appleton and Company, 1915.

Designed as a handbook on the topic of women and trade unions, this work is interesting for the similarity of problems it touches with the questions that are currently relevant.

Troisgros, Simone, and Marcelle Duhareng, "General Report on Trade Unionism and the Employment of Women," in OECD, *Employment of Women*. Paris: 1971.

This report is the result of one of the seminars held in Paris on the employment and earnings of women throughout the world.

Women and Poverty

Goodwin, Leonard, "Welfare Mothers and the Work Ethic," *Monthly Labor Review*, vol. 95, no. 8, August 1972, pp. 35-37.

Even long-term welfare mothers and their teenage sons continue to have a strong work ethic and do not need to be taught the importance of work.

Levinson, Perry, "How Employable Are AFDC Women?" *Welfare in Review*, vol. 8, April-August 1970, pp.12-16.

Employability is measured in terms of two aspects: employment potential, which sums up the abilities and background of the individual, and employment barriers, which measure the conditions which would keep a mother on welfare from applying for a job. On the basis of his study, the author reaches the conclusion that the employment potential of AFDC mothers has risen during the sixties but barriers have not been reduced. Several other articles on the employability of women on welfare have been published in the same review.

Murray, Pauli, "The Negro Woman's Stake in the Equal Rights Amendment," *Harvard Civil Rights—Civil Liberties Law Review*, vol. 6, no. 2, March 1971, pp. 253-59.

Negro women are victimized both on account of race and on account of sex. They remain the most disadvantaged group in the United States.

Stein, Robert L., "The Economic Status of Families Headed by Women," *Monthly Labor Review*, vol. 93, no. 12, December 1970, pp. 3-10.

A description of the income and employment problems of families headed by women. Despite government programs, 2 of the 5.6 million such families remain in poverty.

U.S. Department of Labor, Women's Bureau, *Women in Poverty: Jobs and the Need for Jobs*. Washington: U.S. Government Printing Office, 1968.

About 11.2 million women 16 years old and over experienced poverty in 1966. Of these, 1.8 million were heads of families. Most of them needed and wanted work but were unable to find it. Some were poor even though they had a job. The pamphlet is a statistical treatment of the question of women in poverty.

Willacy, Hazel M., and Harvey J. Hilaski, "Working Women in Urban Poverty Neighborhoods," *Monthly Labor Review*, vol. 93, no. 6, June 1970, pp. 35-38.

The importance of work and the level of wage for women in urban poverty neighborhood is particularly critical. The author presents a statistical profile of the patterns of employment and earnings of the poor woman in urban centers.

Action Programs

American Society for Personnel Administration and Bureau of National Affairs, *ASPA-BNA Survey: Employment of Women*. Washington: 1970.

150 executives were surveyed. The results show that very few women reach executive positions in companies. The study covers company programs to foster the effective utilization of women.

Anderson, Stephen D., and Nancy E. Anderson, "Human Relations Training for Women," *Training and Development*, vol. 25, no. 8, August 1971, pp. 24-27.

The impact of a human relations seminar conducted for female employees (secretaries) at Dow Chemical Company are presented. The general conclusion is that training programs, traditionally reserved for men, can be usefully extended to women.

Berry, Jane, et al., *Guide for Development of Permanent and Part-Time Employment Opportunities for Girls and Women*. Kansas City: University of Missouri-Kansas City, 1969.

An extensive study of part-time employment and its history in the United States. The study concludes that attitudes toward part-time employment are changing in business and government.

Dailey, John T., and Clinton A. Neyman, Jr., *Development of a Curriculum and Materials for Teaching Basic Vocational Talents*. Washington: George Washington University, July 1967.

The study demonstrates that performance on tests of aptitude or vocational talents (whether verbal, nonverbal, or even mechanical) depends on exposure and that it can be effectively improved by training within the public school systems. The authors find useful application for developing such learning opportunities in reducing differences in skills that follow sex or background lines.

DeCrow, Karen, "The Outer World Is Where the Fun Is," *The Young Woman's Guide to Liberation*. New York: Bobbs-Merrill, 1971, pp. 181-96.

The article examines all angles of woman's economic position. Women are encouraged to remain home and barred from high-level positions. Though they own about half the wealth of society, they have little control over their share. Women who are not supported by their husbands must depend on a male-run welfare system. The tax structure in America is heavily biased in favor of men.

Eyde, Lorraine D., "The Status of Women in State and Local Government," paper presented at the International Conference of the Public Personnel Association, San Francisco, California, November 1971.

The author's main recommendation is that "goals and timetables for women in affirmative action plans" and "mechanisms for reviewing progress" should be devised within state and local government units.

Freedman, Marcia, "Poor People and the Distribution of Job Opportunities," *Journal of Social Issues* vol. 26, no. 3, Summer 1970, pp. 35-46.

Economic inequality is not integrated in government decisions and legislation regarding efficiency, growth, and inflation. The economy is divided into large bureaucratized monopolistic sector and a competitive sector of small firms. The center constitutes a complex private welfare state and is expanding at a very fast rate. But small firms, which employ the largest proportion of disadvantaged groups such as blacks and women, are lagging behind.

Galbraith, John Kenneth, Edwin Kuh, and Lester C. Thurow, "The Galbraith Plan to Promote the Minorities," *New York Times Magazine*, August 22, 1971, pp. 9-12.

This article describes Galbraith's program to promote the economic status of minorities. The Minorities Advancement Plan would force large firms to employ minorities and women in the proportion in which they are represented in the labor force of the community. Firms would be given ten to thirteen years to reach this goal.

Ickeringill, Nan, "While Mother Works, the Company Takes Care of the Children," *The New York Times*, August 26, 1970, p. 46.

Business executives are reporting positive results from programs to provide day-care services.

Interdepartmental Committee on the Status of Women and Citizens' Advisory Council on the Status of Women. *1968: Time for Action*. Washington: U.S. Government Printing Office, 1969.

The report contains "highlights of the fourth national Conference of Commissions on the Status of Women." It outlines recommendations as to what commissions can do to improve employment opportunities, promote day-care services, and encourage women to seek top-level positions.

Jensen, Jerry J., "The Supervisor's Key Role in Fair Employment," *Personnel*, vol. 46, no. 2, March/April 1969, pp. 29-33.

The first-line supervisor is the key link in the success of a firm's fair-employment program. New responsibilities fall upon him with the inception of such a program and he should be fully trained and assisted with more than general policy directives.

Killian, Ray A., *The Working Woman*. American Management Association, 1971.
Text presents guidelines for businesses toward the more effective utilization of women.

Klein, Viola, *Women Workers*. Paris: OECD, 1965.
A discussion of the special needs and of the employment practices with regard to women workers in 21 countries. The report contains numerous recommendations (day-care centers, part-time work, etc.) to improve opportunities for women.

Kuttner, Robert L., "The Rusty Fair Employment Machine," *Washington Monthly*, vol. 1, no. 3, April 1969, pp. 62-73.
Without a decision from the White House to make contract compliance a top priority, discriminatory firms will continue to be awarded U.S. government contracts. The agencies that should enforce compliance are timid and understaffed and sanctions are not imposed.

Lambright, W. Henry, "Womanpower: The Next Step in Manpower Policy," *Public Personnel Review*, vol. 31, no. 1, January 1970, pp. 27-30.
The importance of human resources justifies a reexamination of our manpower programs. Scarcities in technical and professional fields in particular must be taken into consideration. The article suggests that the potential of women in these fields is considerable but cannot be fully utilized until discrimination is eliminated.

Low, Seth, and Pearl G. Spindler, *Child-Care Arrangements of Working Mothers in the U.S.*. Children's Bureau, Publication No. 461. Washington: U.S. Government Printing Office, 1968.
One of several publications by the Children's Bureau on child-care centers for the working mothers.

Markoff, Helene S., "The Federal Woman's Program," *Public Administration Review*, vol. 32, March-April 1972, pp. 144-51.
This article discusses the federal women's program which is an action program established to enhance employment and advancement opportunities for women in the federal government.

Mead, Margaret, "Women in National Service," *Teachers College Record*, vol. 73, no. 1, September 1971, pp. 59-64.
The arrogation of any activity wholly to one of the sexes has never had good results. In particular, women need to be freely admitted in a national service, whether it is voluntary or compulsory.

Munts, Raymond, and David C. Rice, "Women Workers: Protection or Equality," *Industrial and Labor Relations Review*, vol. 24, no. 1, October 1970, pp. 3-13.
In banning sex discrimination in employment, Title VII of the Civil Rights

Act poses a serious threat to state legislation designed to protect women against long hours and poor work conditions. To treat all restrictions as discriminatory and to remove them would leave the determination of employment conditions to the free market, a very risky prospect.

National Association of Manufacturers and Plans for Progress, *EEO: Compliance and Affirmative Action*. Washington: National Association of Manufacturers, 1970.

A study of companies' federal contract regulations and compliance.

Orth, Charles D., III, and Frederic Jacobs, "Women in Management: Pattern for Change," *Harvard Business Review*, July/August 1971, pp. 139-47.

Once top management has committed itself to action, numerous paths are available to improve opportunities for women. An organizational appraisal by outsiders is the first step called for, since problems will vary from company to company. This evaluation should be followed by recommendations for innovations in such areas as recruiting practices, training programs, benefit programs, working hours, and day-care facilities.

Rossi, Alice S., "Job Discrimination and What Women Can Do About It," *Atlantic*, vol. 225, no. 3, March 1970, pp. 99-102.

The author proposes two amendments to Title VII: eliminate the current exemption of teachers and include a prohibition of discrimination according to marital status.

Seear, B.N., *Re-entry of Women to the Labor Market After an Interruption in Employment*. Paris: OECD, 1971.

The majority of married women reenter the labor market with no training and indefinite career objectives. Vocational guidance programs must be instituted to encourage women to enter the technical fields in which scarcities will become more serious in the future.

Silverberg, Marjorie M., and Lorraine D. Eyde, "Career Part-time Employment: Personnel Implications of the HEW Professional and Executive Corps," *Good Government*, vol. 88, no. 3, Fall 1971, pp. 11-19.

Positive results were obtained from the HEW demonstration project designed to create less-than-full-time career positions for married women. This and other alternative schemes are discussed as means to promote equal employment opportunity for married women and to reduce waste of manpower.

Task Force of Labor Standards, *Report to the Citizens' Advisory Council on the Status of Women, 1968*. Washington: Government Printing Office, 1968.

The purpose of the study is "to consider the relationship of protective labor legislation to Title VII and to review the effectiveness and role of protective legislation in today's economy."

Task Force on Social Insurance and Taxes, *Report to the Citizens' Advisory Council on the Status of Women, 1968*. Washington: U.S. Government Printing Office, 1968.

The report focuses on two topics. First, social insurance against temporary and long-term wage loss risks: under this heading, the task force examines the unemployment and disability insurance programs and the Social Security Program. Second, working women and the federal income tax.

U.S. Department of Labor, Women's Bureau, *Continuing Education Programs and Services for Women*. Washington: U.S. Government Printing Office, 1971.

A list of 450 programs of educational and other institutions for adult women seeking educational opportunities. This represents a considerable increase over the 250 listed in 1968.

U.S. Department of Labor, Women's Bureau and Personnel and Industrial Relations Association, Inc., *Sex Discrimination in Employment Practices: A Report from the Conference Held at the University of California at Los Angeles in Cooperation with Personnel and Industrial Relations Association, Inc. and the Women's Bureau, September 19, 1968*. Washington: U.S. Government Printing Office, 1970.

Several chapters discuss the current position of women in the labor force. The focus of the conference, however, was on compliance policies and procedures for business and industry.

Williamson, John, "Welfare Policy and Population Policy: A Conflict in Goals," *Urban and Social Change Review*, vol. 4, no. 1, Fall 1970, pp. 21-23.

Two objectives of policy, child support and family planning, must be better integrated in our welfare programs. Both the present AFDC program and Nixon's Family Assistance Plan encourage families to have children.

Zamoff, Richard B., and Jerolyn R. Lyle, *Assessment of Day Care Services and Needs at the Community Level: Mt. Pleasant*. Washington: The Urban Institute, November 1971.

A pilot study assessing needs, preferences, use patterns, and costs of day care in a community within the Washington, D.C. SMSA.

Zapoleon, Marguerite W., *Occupational Planning for Women*. New York: Harper and Brothers, 1961.

The author discusses the need for vocational counseling for women. Guidelines are presented for women and their counselors.

The Legal Point of View

Brown, B.A., Emerson, F.S., Falk, G., and Freedman, A.E., "The Equal Rights Amendment: A Constitutional Basis for Equal Rights for Women," *Yale Law Journal*, vol. 80, no. 5, April 1971, pp. 872-985.

This article discusses the grounds for an equal rights amendment. In developing the case, historical discrimination is discussed in showing how courts have ruled against women.

Brown, B.A., et al., "Civil Rights Act of 1964: An Exception to Prohibitions on

Employment Discrimination," *Iowa Law Journal*, vol. 55, no. 3, December 1969, pp. 509-19.

This note covers the problems of sex discrimination in relation to Title VII as an alternative to the equal-protection clause of the constitution.

Brown, B.A., et al., "Employment Discrimination and Title VII of the Civil Rights Act of 1964," *Harvard Law Review*, vol. 84, no. 6, March 1971, pp. 1109-80.

This note gives an excellent review of the development of Title VII by the EEOC. It treats the problems inherent in interpretation of the Title and getting such interpretations through the courts.

Bureau of National Affairs, "The Equal Employment Opportunity Act of 1972," A Special BNA Report. Washington, D.C.: Bureau of National Affairs, Inc., 1972.

Coverage of the 1964 Civil Rights Act was extended to managers, professionals, teachers, professors, and government employees.

"Current Information Combatting Sex Discrimination in the United States," *International Labor Review*, vol. 106, July-December 1972, pp. 269-72.

Title VII of the Civil Rights Act of 1964 and other protective legislation for women in the U.S. is discussed.

Fox, Harrison William, ed., *Contemporary Issues in Civil Rights and Liberties*. New York: MSS Educational Publishing Co., 1972.

Section I of this collection contains articles dealing with the equal rights amendment to the U.S. Constitution, legal stereotypes of women, and abortion.

Fuentes, S.P., "Federal Remedial Sanctions: Focus on Title VII," *Valpariso Law Review*, vol. 5, no. 2, May 1971, pp. 203-60.

This article gives an area by area discussion of action taken under Title VII.

Kanowitz, L., "Constitutional Aspects of Sex-Based Discrimination in American Law," *Nebraska Law Review*, vol. 48, no. 1, November 1968, pp. 131-82.

This article develops court discrimination under the common-law tradition.

Kanowitz, L., *Women and the Law: The Unfinished Revolution*. Albuquerque: University of New Mexico Press, 1969.

A complete discussion of discrimination against women in terms of both Title VII and the Fourteenth Amendment.

Kanowitz, L., *Laws on Sex Discrimination in Employment: Federal Civil Rights Act, Title VII, State Fair Employment Practices Laws, Executive Orders*, Washington: U.S. Department of Labor, 1970.

A short discussion of the laws and what they say.

Oldham, "Sex Discrimination and State Protective Laws," *Denver Law Journal*, vol. 44, no. 3, Summer 1967, pp. 344-76.

This article provides a good discussion of the problems faced by the EEOC in the conflict between federal and state laws.

Oldham, "Sex Discrimination in Employment: An Attempt to Interpret Title VII of the Civil Rights Act of 1964," *Duke Law Journal*, vol. 1968, no. 4, August 1968, pp. 671-723.

Discusses problems encountered under Title VII through 1968. Emphasis is on interpretation of bona fide occupational qualification.

Oldham, "A Woman's Place: Diminishing Justification for Sex Discrimination," *Southern California Law Review*, vol. 42, 1968-69, pp. 183-211.

A good discussion of problems in Title VII in terms of implementing that section.

Oldham, *1969 Handbook on Women Workers*. Washington: U.S. Department of Labor, 1969.

This book provides excellent background material as to just what is the status of women workers in our society.

Index

159

About the Authors

Jerolyn R. Lyle received the Ph.D. in economics from the University of Maryland in 1970. She has served as staff economist for the U.S. Office of Education and as senior economist for the U.S. Equal Employment Opportunity Commission. She has been an economic consultant with the U.S. Office of Management and Budget and with the Urban Institute. After teaching at Smith College, she joined the faculty of the American University in 1971. She has written widely in the field of manpower economics.

Jane L. Ross received the Ph.D. from the American University in economics in 1972. She served as staff economist in the Office of Economic Opportunity and in the office of the Assistant Secretary for Planning in the U.S. Department of Health, Education and Welfare. She has done quantitative research in economic development as well as in manpower economics.